FARM YAR[D]

C000258751

David Storey

Cartoons: Rupert Besley

Published by Atlantic Publishers, Holebottom Farm, Hebden, Skipton, North Yorkshire, BD23 5DL.

ISBN: 0 906899 97 4

First published 1999

© David Storey, 1999

Design and layout: Trevor Ridley
Printed by The Amadeus Press Ltd., Huddersfield, West Yorkshire

All rights reserved. No part of this publication may be reproduced, stored in a retrieval system, or transmitted, in any form or by any means, electronic, mechanical, photocopying, recording or otherwise, without prior permission in writing from the publishers.

British Cataloguing in Publication Data
A catalogue record for this book is available from the British Library.

CONTENTS

INTRODUCTION

To breakfast upon one of your own hen's freshly laid eggs while looking at your contented calves grazing peacefully in your lush green meadow is the idyllic dream of many who enjoy a Sunday afternoon drive in the countryside. But dreams can be as elusive as that full egg cup.

For a start your hens may not be laying. At least not in a place where the eggs can be readily found. And your calves may have been busy since dawn trampling down a field of barley belonging to your most difficult neighbour – the one with no discernible sense of humour.

Your crop of golden coloured hay was drying out nicely. Which makes last night's downpour all the more annoying. And of course the wretched goat, which you only keep for the sake of the children, has broken free from her tether again and taken off to the next parish. Before the day gets much older you can be sure of an angry phone call to inform you of her precise whereabouts and the number of gardens she has eaten. In fact the only creatures in view are a large flock of crows who have ignored your elaborate Rambo scarecrow to feast on your field of ripening strawberries.

You have a few well-finished cattle for sale at the moment. But the man on the radio won't stop talking about BSE. So prices will be down even further. Changes in farming can be dramatic. It's not so long ago since it was only bulls that were thought to be mad. Now it's the cows as well.

The Americans have the right idea. Instead of living in the country, they buy a video of carefully selected pastoral scenes and have it on all day on gigantic screens in their downtown apartments. Of course they are careful not to include footage of a rampant fox in the hen house or of a sheep crawling with maggots. And they certainly don't show action pictures of turkeys being slaughtered for Christmas. But I'd settle for the video if I thought my animals would leave me alone long enough to watch it.

However, the other man's grass is always greener. Especially to those who live in crowded urban areas with no grass at all. There are two things you need if you live in the country – a good pair of waterproof boots and a well-developed sense of humour. The boots can be readily bought but the sense of humour has to be acquired. In the development of the latter you will be greatly assisted by your animals.

Whether it's a simple matter of moving your cattle from one field to the next or the more complicated business of persuading

your ewes not to lamb during an international rugby match, your animals will never take you seriously. Fortunately my therapist assures me that this has little to do with any shortcomings I might have as a farmer. It's more to do with the nature of animals and of farming itself – the oldest and most ridiculous profession in the world.

1
A WOOLLY SENSE OF TIMING

Having animals of any kind is an even worse tie than having children. At least with children, if you want to go away for a weekend you do have the choice, however dubious, of taking them with you. And if all you have is a pet dog or cat then you may have some chance of being allowed to take them with you wherever you go. But farm animals such as hens or sheep are unlikely to be the recipients of such tolerant invitations.

At the best of times if you go away you will have to prevail on some kind neighbour to come in and feed the stock. But there are times when you just can't leave them at all. With sheep, lambing is one such time. Therefore it make sense to time your lambing so that important occasions such as Christmas and the New year are free for socialising. Those of us who chose to live in under populated areas need to actively guard our level of social activity.

The festive season is one example of a time that is particularly unsuitable for lambing. Even the most obsessive of farmers would rather be sipping brandy by the fire than keeping watch in a cold sheep shed. Given that the date any ewe gives birth depends on when she mates with her male partner, it ought to be a simple matter to subtract 147 days from the dates that lambing would be undesirable and ensure that the ram is well away from the ewes during that period. Unfortunately such a scientific approach takes no account of the whereabouts of the neighbour's rams or the condition of his fences. As a result an extraordinary number of lambs are born on public holidays.

Very few sheep lamb between nine in the morning and five in the evening, that is, during normal working hours. They have a preference for daybreak or the middle of the night. Regular sleep and shepherding are no more compatible now than they were in biblical times. Otherwise, it might have been left to office workers to notice the first coming.

Apart from the middle of the night another favourite time for lambing is Saturday afternoons. This is especially true if there is a rugby match on. Rugby matches are short, lasting no more than an hour and a half, but rarely is it possible to reach the final score of a five nations match without having to attend to a mother to be. Oddly enough, they have a curious preference for matches against Wales. Once I even tried talking to the sheep before the kick off (who can say what they understand?) pleading with them to either lamb now or wait till after the final whistle. Few will be surprised to hear that my request was ignored.

An equally popular time for lambing is when there are guests for dinner. Our mainly urban friends invariably express the wish to observe the miracle of birth. And, being heavily fortified on the wine they have brought, one rarely has the courage or the wit to refuse them. Memories of a previous highly strung female guest going home in tears when a new born lamb displayed a complete lack of enthusiasm for breathing in and out, seldom surface on such occasions. So boots are found and they all march excitedly to the sheep house expressing the usual surprise at the sheer quantity of muck on the way.

While shepherds watched...

sucking contentedly on his mother, the conversation generally turns to the joys and advantages of farming life. The standard comments about living in harmony with nature, being free from the stresses of urban life and having a plentiful supply of healthy home-produced food are made. It's usually at the mention of food or very soon afterwards that it dawns on one of the visitors that they have just eaten the new born lamb's older sister or at the very least, a close cousin. It's then that some tearful guest who only an hour earlier was happy to eat considerably more than an average sized helping of home-produced lamb will hold his or her substantial stomach as if they had somehow ingested a live hand grenade. All frantic attempts to console the guest by pointing out that their dinner had enjoyed a very happy life on our organic farm or by arguing (logically in my view) that vegetables are living things as well, are met with blank and troubled stares. The guests look at me in a manner similar to the way the disciples must have looked at Judas.

At such moments I can be certain that the final party-stopping question is about to be asked. There is no longer any danger of my guests overstaying their welcome, an early night is in store for all. And sure enough out it comes, on cue, the one sentence guaranteed to alter my natural disposition as a kind and considerate host. Looking at me with a mixture of contempt and pity somebody asks 'How can you eat your own animals?'

Last year, to avoid any disruption of the festive season the ram was not allowed near the ewes until the middle of October. Thus there would be no lambing until March. Considerable time was also spent checking the fences lest any neighbour's ram gained access to our field of healthy females. We looked forward to a peaceful Christmas and New Year and made plans for enjoying the extra free time we would have.

The change to March lambing was definitely a good move. The festive season was much more enjoyable than before. And we only had three lambs born on Christmas Day compared with five the year before.

I don't consider myself an expert on sheep husbandry. But I have learned that the last thing you need when placing your hand inside a ewe's womb is some urban yuppy to say 'Oh! I hope you are not hurting the poor thing'. Everything goes downhill after that. Invariably that sentence, which never fails to rise me, ensures that the birth of the lamb in question will be as difficult as it will be messy. The confidence of the audience in my ability to successfully deliver the lamb wanes dramatically as I fumble around inside the ewe for heads and legs.

When I have finally convinced myself that I am not dealing with the nightmare of a five legged lamb and the creature is being ever so carefully eased into the world, I can be sure of that second infuriating sentence from my guests. 'I hope you are not pulling too hard'. By this stage I am so angry that when the lamb arrives I make a point of slapping him hard, swinging him in a circle over my head before dropping him into a bucket of icy water, even if he is breathing perfectly normally on arrival. My ability to confine my reaction to such a mild display of irritation, may be taken as conclusive evidence that living in the country is at least as good as regular valium.

Back at the dinner table, having left the new born lamb

2
MENDING FENCES

It is said that 'good neighbours make good fences'. Or is it 'good fences make good neighbours?' Either way, keeping your animals in and those of your neighbour's out is a constant preoccupation of all but the most super-efficient farmers. Getting on with your neighbours is vital in the country as you can't change them without moving your farm.

No less than people, animals like the adventure of travel and the thrill of discovering new places. They get bored with their own surroundings and literally long for greener pastures. Hence the need for secure stock-proof fencing.

Prickly bushes are a traditional way of keeping the animals at home. Simply stuffing a big thorny bush into a gap in the hedgerow is a quick and easy solution to a potential outbreak. Gorse and hawthorn are the best type to use – no animal likes sticking his face into them. At the other end of the scale is the ivy bush which is no use at all. Animals love it, so they will be delighted to eat their way through it and out of the field. Wire fencing, electrified or otherwise is probably the most secure and permanent solution to straying stock. But if the animals are sufficiently excited they can tear their way through that too.

Animals generally break out when their owner is in his good clothes and about to go out. Faced with this situation, the farmer can either go back to the house and change into his boots and working clothes in which case he will be late for whatever he is going to. Or he can take a chance that he will manage to run them back without get-

ting dirty. Of course experience should tell him that is not a viable option. Animals have no respect for suits. They see enough of them on butchers and meat factory buyers at the market.

How fussy you have to be about your fencing depends on the kind of neighbour you have. If he is the sort whose own animals never ever get out and who will pick up the phone the minute he sees an extra lamb in his fields, then you need to be fairly thorough with your boundaries. At least with the ones which bound his land. There is nothing worse than having to leave the dinner table on account of an awkward neighbour. Happily most farmers take a more pragmatic view of visiting

Please can we have our bull back?

Actually I've opened it all up as footpaths this winter — it's saved me no end of ploughing!

animals. They tend not to complain too readily, as they know from experience that as soon as they do complain to you, their own animals will be off and into your fields.

Sheep always have an eye on the next field. After all, they belong on the mountains where they can roam freely and unhindered. It only takes one sheep to find a way out and, true to their reputation, all the others will follow. If you can identify the one or two rogues in your flock whose lives are devoted to escaping and get rid of them, then your life will be a lot more peaceful. Some sheep will never stay easy until they are safely on a plate.

Cattle are much more passive animals. But of course being bigger, they can force their way through almost anything if excited or frightened. It's nothing to an energetic bullock to trample down a few hours of fencing work in a matter of seconds and tear off down the road with yards of wire and bushes trailing behind him. And you can be sure you'll never manage to shoo him out of your neighbour's garden without being seen.

Goats are easily the worst of all. Apart from the fact that they are almost impossible to catch, once out they can do untold damage. A neighour's goat recently succeeded in getting into his house. Which of his children left the front door open has not yet been determined although investigations are still ongoing. Anyway, before being discovered, the goat managed to eat two sets of curtains and part of the corner of a recently purchased carpet. Needless to say it was on that very day that the neighbour decided he could live very well without fresh goats' milk.

Fortunately there is more to being a good neighbour than making good fences. Otherwise, very few of us could ever hope to make the grade.

3
PATRONS OF THE MARTS

For farmers, a day at the mart is a bit like a day at the races. There, animals are bought and sold with the same intensity and excitement you'd expect to find at any big race meeting. To sprawling expanses of unappealing concrete and iron buildings are brought the prize heifers, the champion rams, and the fattest pigs from the surrounding farms and beyond. In lorries and trailers of all sizes and varying states of repair, from dilapidated wooden trailers to gleaming red lorries, farmers bring the fruits of their labours, to claim their just financial rewards. Here, the lonely nights spent delivering new born lambs, the endless repairing of fences to restrain energetic young bulls, or the drudgery of continually 'mucking out' the pig house will be rewarded. Like the trainer at the race course, the farmer parades his animals in the ring hoping for the jackpot.

Unlike a racecourse, the mart was not built with the comfort of its patrons in mind. There are no Pullman seats, only hard wooden benches which are marked with the dirt of thousands

of farmers' boots which have rested on them over the years. There used to be a bar there, but as frequently buyers, sellers and even animals stayed in there singing endless choruses of 'Old McDonald' when they should have been in the sales ring, the service was suspended.

The mart does have a canteen. Those readers who, like myself, have often wondered about the precise difference between a restaurant and a canteen will have their long standing confusion resolved after a meal in the mart canteen. For despite the fact that at any given moment there are tons of good healthy food being paraded around the nearby sales ring, none of it seems to end up in the canteen. It's hard to believe that any of the dishes on offer there ever made it to the mart under their own steam.

The auctioneer, who clearly has no need of a speed reading course – his words per minute would be the envy of any typist-

supervises the bidding as the animals are paraded in the ring. The seller stands in a booth similar to a phone box beside the auctioneer and indicates his acceptance or rejection of the final bid. This is generally done with a slight shake of the head or a gentle waving of the thumb.

The box, as it is called, has a window at the top but not at the bottom. This feature allows farmers who do not wish buyers to know who is selling, to avoid discovery by sitting on the floor of the box or crouching below the top window. To be certain of anonymity a few farmers enter the box on all fours. Why some patrons of the mart feel the need to keep their identity a secret has never been adequately explained to me.

It may be that in the past they managed to pass off some weak or sickly animals on some unsuspecting factory buyer, and don't wish to be remembered for it. Alternatively they may believe that the local inspector of taxes is present.

It has certainly nothing to do with women, as the attendance at the mart is as male as any esoteric secret society. Whatever their reasons, the spectacle of grown men entering the box in the same manner as their animals enter the ring is just one intriguing aspect of a visit to the mart.

It is said that those who work with animals eventually come to resemble them in character and appearance. This theory is often advanced as a reason for keeping away from women who breed dogs. My natural scepticism of this proposition was severely tested after a few hours of observing the clientele at the local mart. There is definitely something in it, most noticeably among the pig breeders. A significant proportion of these men are small and rounded with a tendency to be red-faced and excitable, thick bodied men and fat, not unlike the rashers that their animals will soon become. Sheep breeders on the other hand tend to be thin and willowy, perhaps a result of many years spent chasing their errant animals up and down the mountains. Worried looking men, they dart about like a numerically deficient ewe who is having difficulty accounting for each of her triplets.

Any heavily built individual striding slowly round the ring with a marked air of confidence is more than likely to be a successful cattle dealer. His purposeful strides are reminiscent of a favourite cow making her way to her own special place in the milking parlour. As men who control beasts heavier than themselves, they have good reason to walk taller than the rest. Obviously such observations fall far short of acceptable scientific investigation, but the notion that farmers become like the animals they work with is worthy of further investigation. Whether such a theory has any application for vegetable growers or snail farmers is beyond the scope of this initial study.

For many readers a mart may merely be an animal market but for the student of human sciences it can also be a rich source of research material. If you've never been before then why not make a day of it? But keep your head straight and your hands in your pockets. Otherwise, you might have to bring home half a dozen heifers in the boot of your car.

4
A HAPPY FARMER?

There is a man who lives a few miles away from me who says he's happy. Where he lives never struck me before as a place of unlimited bliss. The land is rough and his house is a long way from any pretence of civilisation. Only the foolhardy would attempt to drive their car up his lane. Even the postman would only make the bumpy journey when he had

Agreed, there's no actual sign to say No Parking here –

accumulated a good fistful of post. However, the clever individual solved that problem by ordering the daily newspaper for himself.

But a more peculiar fact about this happy man is that he is a farmer. A farmer who says he's happy? When did you last hear of such a thing? Farmers are put on this world to moan and complain and demand that the government/EEC/weatherman/taxman etc. give them a secure living. A farmer who goes around claiming to be happy is letting us all down. In fact he's a danger to the entire industry. Happy people are never given grants. The whole point of grants is to reduce unhappiness. Grants are a means of redistributing the national supply of well being. So happy farmers should keep their mouths firmly shut in case they derail the EU gravy train. The train is so unpopular with some urban dwellers that it travels in constant danger of being hijacked. Being such a slow train, it wouldn't take much to stop it altogether.

Actually, to be fair to the farmer, the word he used to describe himself was content. But to the rest of us miserable and disconsolate people it's much the same thing. And it's certainly a long way ahead of most of the rural community at the moment.

Townies

Happy is not the word city people use to describe farmers. At present their opinion of them is only a few points above that of toothaches, litter and insurance sales-man. In many ways farmers have only themselves to blame for this. Being paid for doing nothing and being compensat-ed for low prices will never be popular with consumers no matter how cheap food becomes as a result. Imagine the reaction of the public to shopkeepers if they demanded a grant to compensate them for a fall in the price of jelly babies? Or if hairdressers looked for headage payments? And would people be in favour of paying train drivers for leaving their trains idling at the station?

Old McDonald

On the other hand the public seem quite happy to support Panda bears, tired don-keys and gigantic whales. So why do they have it in so much for the farmers? It must be all down to public relations. We farmers need a better image. Perhaps

That's what I love about living in the country – all this wonderful fruit 'n veg right at one's door!

pictures of contented ewes being fed oats that were bought with the EU ewe premium might soften the hearts of the intol-erant public? Or maybe a few photos of all those millions of rare and exotic plants growing on setaside land might help city people to see that money spent on farmers is money well spent? We could always throw in a few Spice Girl lookalikes singing a rap version of Old McDonald for good measure. Perhaps they could wear T shirts with the slogan 'You'll have nothing to eat if you chew up the farmers'. It certainly couldn't make our image any worse.

Drink

But to get back to our contented farmer. As well as boasting of his happiness, he also told me that he doesn't drink. Perhaps that's the real secret? Perhaps he doesn't actually know what it is to be happy? Having never felt that warm glow of satisfaction that comes from having half a bottle of whisky inside him, how could he possibly know what happi-ness is? Without having experienced that late night feeling

when everybody is your best friend and all women are beauti-ful, how would he recognise happiness? Whatever he claims to feel can hardly be compared to the euphoria of greeting the dawn through the window of your local pub.

Cornflakes

Happiness is a bit like money, something other people always seem to have more of. Although most of them probably have considerably less than we think. But unlike money, the amount of happiness any individual has in his possession can never be measured. However, I suspect that what this man describes as happiness might be no more than the mildly OK feeling you get after eating a bowl of cornflakes? Or it could be similar to the sense of relief you feel when your mother rings to say she won't be visiting you for the holidays after all? With the depressing state of farming today, I think I'm right to be suspicious of this man's happiness. But if he is really happy, then on behalf of all farmers, let me be the first to begrudge it to him. Begrudgery as an art form has always been the preserve of the farmer.

5
HORSELESS CARTS

As an organic farmer with a concern for the environment, it seemed a good idea to invest in a donkey and cart as an ecologically sound mode of transport. Using an animal instead of a tractor would reduce the release of diesel fumes into the atmosphere. As a sustainable form of energy, it would be unaffected by increasing oil prices or by its diminishing supply. And by converting our own grass and hay into transport, our farm would become more self sufficient. Having a donkey would be the environmental equivalent of being politically correct.

'Never satisfied, you farmers, are you?'

The children, of course, were delighted at the prospect of galloping round the fields on her back. Being young, that fine distinction that separates a donkey from a racehorse was not apparent to them. So when our neighbour arrived with the already named Jenny pulling her battered wooden cart, they were already fighting over who would get to ride her first.

It was on the very first ride in the cart that we discovered that Jenny was a very independent animal. Which side of the public road she occupied had more to do with the quality of the leaves on the hedgerows than the highway code. The route she travelled took little account of her passenger's wishes. Her direction seemed to depend on her own assessment of the probability of a particular road having a good supply of grass or tasty bushes. This didn't really matter until it was time to return home. The amount of energy we used persuading, cajoling, and tricking her into going in the required direction, augured badly for her future as an energy saving form of transport.

However, pleasure trips were not the reason we has acquired her and we were happy to attribute her apparent uncooperative nature to the fact that we were strangers to her. It was simply a question of getting to know her and developing some basic form of communication.

She was happy in the field with the cattle although at first her surprisingly loud braying frightened some of the calves. Being early in the year, we were carrying feed to the stock every day and Jenny soon developed an appetite for oats. This was fine in the beginning when she would take her place at the end of the trough and munch along with the rest.

It didn't take her long to realise that she had the ability to frighten the cattle away from the trough and that this meant she could have all the oats to herself. Feeding the cattle, which had hitherto been one of the more pleasant winter tasks, became a major ordeal as it became necessary to remain with the animals while they ate and to constantly chase Jenny away.

Vegetable growers will know just how back breaking much of the work involved in vegetable production can be. Harvesting potatoes tops the list of muscular tasks. This was the main reason for getting a donkey – to bring the potatoes and other heavy vegetables from the field to the vegetable store. So when harvesting time arrived, we hauled the cart out of the shed and prepared Jenny for work. The tackling, an elaborate combination of strings and ropes was tied around her and the cart in numerous permutations until the most logical arrangement was found. In most cases it was the last and most unlikely option that turned out to be the correct one. After several false starts, the point was eventually reached where whenever Jenny moved forward, the cart would follow.

Jenny's function was to pull the cart full of potatoes from the field into the yard a few hundred yards away. She seemed happy to stand still while the cart was loaded and when it was full I led her out of the field at a nice steady pace. After a while she started to go faster which was fine by me as it meant the

job would be finished all the quicker. When she broke into a canter and I had difficulty keeping up with her, I began to worry that the potatoes might fall off. When, for no apparent reason and without any prior warning, she skidded to a complete halt, they did just that. Every single one of them. However, we grudgingly loaded up the cart for the second time and eventually the potatoes reached their destination.

It was on the next load that I began to question the wisdom of having a donkey in the first place. The cart loaded, she refused to budge. And, when, after several minutes of everybody shouting at her and jumping up and down behind her, she took off like a greyhound from a trap I knew her days as an environmentally friendly form of transport were numbered. Defeated, I put her back in the field and rang my neighbour for a loan of his tractor and reflected how the course of Christianity might have been radically altered had Jenny been the chosen donkey in biblical times.

The following season we invested in an old second hand tractor of our own. It belches out a lot of oily smoke and, like Jenny, it can be very noisy and difficult to get started. But it's great when it gets going, travelling as it does at an even steady pace. A further advantage is the fact that it has no interest whatsoever in oats and we never have to muck out the garage.

And Jenny? She has a great life now. She's fully recovered from her initial introduction to work. However, potato harvesting has apparently had a lasting effect on her as we haven't managed to catch her since. Jenny has become to transport what a cock is to egg laying. She grazes away happily in the field with the cattle and the sheep, braying now and again to remind us and the entire neighbourhood that she is still there. She's a familiar feature of the area now as occasionally she takes herself off up the road to visit the neighbour's gardens. She's got much fatter too. The oats are obviously good for her.

6
HELPING WITH THE HAY

As anyone who has bought a new house will know, for some time after you move in there is a dramatic increase in the number of visitors who call to see you. And if you ever buy a farm, you can be sure that if the house has a doorbell that works, it will be constantly ringing with curious friends eager to see how you are adapting to your newly adopted lifestyle. People with regular salaried employment assume that if you live and work on a farm, you are always free to receive them. And those couples who have taken the rather doubtful step of reproducing themselves, are always looking for ways of entertaining their over-indulged offspring. What could be more pleasant than an afternoon in the country?

The worst part of these unannounced visits is that the visitors always want to give you a hand. They never offer to clean out the hen house or turn the dung heap, jobs that have actually needed doing for months. And they certainly don't want to even look at a maggoty sheep. At this time of the year what they all want to do is help with the hay. This back breaking task which often takes place at a moment's notice and in a state of advanced panic on account of the unreliable weather, invokes the most romantic of misconceptions in those unfamiliar with the vicissitudes of farming life. Having sufficient knowledge of farming by now to know that there is seldom any call for totally unskilled labour on a farm, I generally decline such offers of help.

But in a weak moment, during this summer's unexpected fine spell, I decided it might be a good idea to invite them all to a barbecue on the day of the hay making. Everybody could help to 'stook' the bales, and afterwards we could all celebrate with charcoal steaks. My friends were all delighted at having finally been offered the chance to 'muck in'. Some of them were even old enough to remember summers in the fifties when office workers in towns were let out of work to help the farmers save the hay. They waited anxiously for the announcement that the hay was ready to be saved, frequently ringing me up to make sure that I hadn't forgotten them.

So the helpers dutifully arrived, all dressed up for work. For a minority of practically minded guests this meant shorts or old jeans and runners. However, the majority came more prepared for a party than for working in the fields.

Long summer dresses mingled with expensive sports coats, perfume mingled with aftershave and, as often happens in the slower pace of rural life, the contractor who was to bale the hay mingled too long in a neighbour's field and failed to arrive at the appointed time. The chattering labour force, who looked more like an advertisement for the local boutique than a group of migrant agricultural workers, would have to wait.

Surprisingly, I was able to contact him on his tractor with his new mobile phone. He assured me he would be in my hay field in less than two hours. Familiar with the vagueness with which time is measured in the country and with our guests becoming impatient, I, foolishly as it turned out, decided to proceed with the barbecue and stook the bales afterwards.

Barbecues are great fun, especially when you live in the

country. There are no neighbours to watch what you are eating, comment on what you are wearing or to feel snubbed at not being invited. You can play music as loud as you like and provided you are among friends, be as exuberant as you wish in the warm summer sun. Perhaps that's why people tend to drink a lot at barbecues. This one was no exception.

Three hours later, when the contractor rang to say that tractor and baler were on their way, most of the guests had become rather silly. You know the sort of thing, playing with the children's toys, imitating the hens, or making faces at the cattle in the adjoining field.

Nevertheless, ever optimistic, I led them all to the hay field. Some ladies in high heels had difficulty traversing our potholed lane and one of the men came to grief when he, unwisely, attempted to jump over the metal gate into the field. One glamorous female friend looked like a demure bride on her wedding day as she held her full length summer dress off the ground to prevent it coming into contact with the assorted animal wastes that are to be found on any farmyard lane. It would not be an understatement to describe the mood of the guests as highly exuberant as they awaited the arrival of the baler. They frolicked along like children on a school outing.

I will never forget the face of the tractor driver as he rounded the corner into the field. A decent quiet man, nothing could have prepared him for the sight of twenty overdressed men and women, many with glass in hand, singing and dancing as he manoeuvred his machinery into the field. He was certainly surprised when they all joined hands and marched around his tractor in a circle. I'm sure his natural suspicions of city people like myself who migrate to peaceful rural areas were suitably confirmed that day.

Needless to say the 'stooking' was a disaster. The few guests who didn't find the bales either 'much too heavy' or full of 'those nasty thistles' were completely unable to master the art of standing one bale against another. Others quickly discovered the complete impossibility of holding a wine glass in one hand and lifting a bale with the other. The glamorous female in the long summer dress was immediately in difficulties on account of her especially sensitive fingers, a fact which had completely escaped my notice on the many occasions she graced social evenings with a performance on her piano. She soon absolved herself from the proceedings altogether and went off in search of her hand cream. Seeing one defector, others quickly followed. Some edged themselves gradually towards the gate before disappearing up the lane back to the house, hoping that such a controlled exit might escape my attention. Others strode purposefully out of the field as if to create the impression that they were being called away on a matter of some considerable urgency. A few guests remained, presumably feeling some sense of obligation towards their host.

But it wasn't long before these morally obligated few, rather arrogantly in my view, began to question the purpose of the entire operation. Some of these well-watered guests, all with less than an hour's agricultural experience behind them, even had the audacity to suggest alternative methods of stooking the bales. In the end, as darkness fell on hundreds of 'unstooked' bales, the futile exercise was abandoned.

I resented getting up early the next day to stook the bales alone. After all it was Sunday. Luckily a neighbouring farmer spotted me in the field and came with his children to help. And he was kind enough not to comment on any of the empty glasses or bottles that lay glistening in the morning sun. Since that morning I have developed a great respect for people who, although aware of our follies, are not consumed with the need to point them out.

Actually, we were wondering if you'd mind growing something not quite such a bright yellow —

7
KINGS OF THE FARMYARD

As the lion is king of the jungle, cattle are the kings of the farmyard. This may be because they are bigger than other farm animals. Dealing with animals that are bigger and physically stronger than oneself ensures them of a level of respect not given to smaller stock. They are also more valuable than other farm animals. A good sized beast can be worth more than twenty lambs. Or for those who like figures, more than the value of two hundred laying hens or four thousand butterhead lettuce.

Managing other farm animals is physically easier. That's probably why cattle farmers are taller and stronger than the rest of us. An errant hen can be caught by the legs and carried back to the hen house. A sheep can be held with one hand and given her vitamins with the other. And if you are a snail farmer, then I presume moving your stock is simply a matter of throwing a few hundred into a bucket and carrying them.

Cattle are not as easy to move as anyone who has had one stand on his toe will quickly confirm. And if they stray into your garden, or worse again, that of your neighbour, no matter how quietly you get them out the garden will be ruined.

Despite their deceptively bovine appearance, cattle are considerably more intelligent than other farm animals. Jumping up and down in front of them or making faces at them doesn't impress them very much. To move half a ton of a beast requires more skill than mere bluster.

Contrary to the urban view of the countryside, not every cow in the field is a bull. In fact there are few bulls in the fields these days. Most of them live in sperm banks. Bulls can be downright dangerous animals so most farmers prefer to have their cows artificially inseminated. When the cow comes on heat or is bulling, she is impregnated with sperm that has been kept on ice. Thus, most cows are single mothers. What effect this has on the cow or her offspring has never been studied. Does the cow feel socially stigmatised as she raises her fatherless child? With no male around, is the calf more difficult to discipline? And what's the view of the calf on the matter? Does it spend its life trying to trace its father? Can an all female environment be seen as a balanced family structure for the growing calf, especially during those dangerous pubescent years?

As it's only Americans who see fit to bring their animals to the psychiatrist, we can only speculate as to what long term psychological effects test tube fathers will have on the social development of cattle.

If you are new to cattle and fearful of their size, then it's wise to start with calves. That way, as with children, getting used to their sheer bulk will be a gradual process and all your skills as a cowboy will not be called upon at once.

For every calf you buy you will also need to buy a bucket and a bag of milk-replacer. The latter is a white powder which when diluted in warm water can be stirred back into milk. If the water is not warm enough then the solution will be lumpy like badly made porridge and you will be stirring it for ever. There are no short cuts to successful calf rearing.

Initially you can simply bring the bucket into the calf house,

place it on a level part of the floor and the calf will drink his ration. But before long, the calf will learn that your appearance at the door with bucket in hand signifies food and he will make a lunge for the bucket as soon as he hears you coming. A lot of milk will be spilt this way if you don't have an alternative plan.

One approach is to leave the bucket outside the door and go into the calf house without it. In the house, pretend you have come to tidy his straw or rearrange his hay. Busy yourself with any non feeding activity. Whistle a few tunes to give the impression of a man casually passing the time. Bring a newspaper if you like. Then when the calf is eventually fooled into thinking that feeding time is not due and is not watching you, open the door quickly with one hand, grab the bucket with the other and swing it into its place on the floor of the house. It's vital that this operation is carried out in one swift movement before the calf realises what's happening. Any hesitation on your part and the calf will make a lunge when the bucket of milk is in mid air and all will be lost. As speed is so essential to the success of this diversionary tactic, its worth practising the tech-

nique in an empty shed for a few days first. Of course you don't have to use real milk when practising. Waste oil is a perfect substitute.

The great disadvantage of this method of avoiding spilt milk is the amount of time it takes. A simpler method is to place the bucket outside the shed and let the calf out to feed. But unless it's raining heavily the big problem with this method is the difficulty of getting the reluctant calf back into the shed.

With calves, as with all farm animals, it's imperative to avoid the temptation of giving him or her a name. Unless you are rich enough to afford to run your farm as an ever expanding zoo, you will be raising animals whose final destination will be a plate. To lessen the moral minefield that this fact invokes and also to be sure you can eat your own dinner, names should be avoided. Believe me, it's a lot easier to eat a sirloin steak than it is to digest a Julio or a Matilda.

One solution is to give all your animals the same name. That way, you never know exactly which Susie is in your stew. But having every sheep, calf, hen and whatever else you might have,

Coo, it works an' all !

coming to you every time you call one of them, greatly miti-gates against the running of a well-ordered farm.

A little known fact about cattle is that they can swim. (Although a few farmers who graze their stock on islands have known this for years.) Of course they can't do the back-stoke but their surprisingly graceful bovine belly flop will be quickly demonstrated if you have a field that bounds a river and are unwise enough to think that the water course does not require fencing. In fact if you are a non-swimmer, it would be advis-able not to buy land with anything deeper than a shallow stream. Even if you do swim, you're probably not that keen on putting your togs on in December.

The hardest part of raising cattle is having to face the day when they are sold. Even without names they quickly become your friends. And to sell your friends is to betray them. It's even more difficult if you have children. While they are still small you can tell them that your cattle have gone to live with another kind farmer. Or that you gave them away to keep some lonely old cow company. But as they get older the stark truth will out. When this happens you can be sure that you alone will be blamed for centuries of animal slaughter and that your off-spring will immediately become vegetarians and militant ani-mals rights activists. And move out.

8
RURAL WORRY

Town dwellers are always telling me how lucky I am to be living in the country. The reason for my good fortune, they inform me, is lack of stress. Apparently, anyone who lives in the middle of a few green fields is immune to this new and very trendy ailment. Stress is therefore a rather mysterious ailment that can effect anyone who doesn't live in the country. It attacks city dwellers indiscriminately and without warning. Although it's possible to catch it in the open air, particularly where there is heavy traffic, it's more likely to attack you if you have a big important job in an office in the city. The bigger the job, the higher the level of stress. While not a lot is known about the origin of this new disease, its favourite breeding ground seems to be high rise office buildings, government departments, and the head offices of anything. It appears to multiply rapidly in any building that has a fax machine. In fact some of these places have become so infested with the disease that it's now possible to get it by fax.

Many of these unfortunate urban dwellers are so deeply infected by stress that they have to attend long and extremely expensive courses to help them recover. On these courses, facilitators and chairpeople with years of stressful experiences behind them, explain in horrifying and frequently embarrassing detail how they overcame their darkest moments. And how the experience has transformed them into the touchy feely meditating candle burning types they have become today. Then, after a herbal tea break, the students are taught how to breathe in and out, how to sit comfortably on a chair, how to sleep soundly

I told him not to go out with that terrible cough-

CROSSING THE NORTH-SOUTH DIVIDE

and how to talk to people. On the more advanced courses, these unhappy 'refugees from reality' learn how to 'get in touch with their true selves', a subject unlikely to attract much of an attendance outside the major cities. Except perhaps in some of the more extreme experiments in community living that take place well away from main roads.

Of course this ever so interesting new condition is just a fancy word for good old-fashioned worry. Worrying is something we do very well in the country. We worry about whether our friends will bring their grossly overparented children with them the next time they visit and frighten the life out of our hens again. We worry about whether it was the smell of pig slurry on our shoes that ended the last dinner party so abruptly.

Or if it was my inability to refrain from commenting on our host's children's extraordinary late bedtimes, particularly the small ginger haired wailer that put his hand in my soup?

We worry when our animals are sick. We worry even more when they die. If the price of lamb falls or the beef subsidy is late or the grass won't grow or the weather is bad, or the young lad is on drugs – we worry. Contrary to the populist urban belief, a peaceful landscape is no guarantee of a stress-free existence. In fact our relaxed rural lifestyle probably leaves us more time for worrying.

Perhaps it's time to start courses in 'How to Cope With Rural Worry'. Provided it wasn't compulsory to drink the herbal tea, we might be happy to learn how to sit comfortably in a chair while our best cow dies. Or how to sleep soundly while our ewes are having triplets. They might show us how to talk to our neighbour while our goats are busy destroying his field of barley. Or better still, how to sleep soundly on top of the mountain of forms we get from the E.U. On the advanced course they might even teach us how to let the whole farm go to pot.

Of course they'd have to teach the animals not to worry as well. Or more importantly, not to worry us. They'd have to teach them to stay calm when we forget to feed them. Stop them bellowing for the vet every time they get a little pain in their stomach. Teach them not to baa for us everytime they find themselves one lamb short of a triplet.

Of course if you are rich enough you don't have to worry. You can pay someone else to do it for you. The big farmers around here pay a man in in the nearest town a monthly rate to do all their worrying. That's why they all look so relaxed. And the man in the town is happy too. He never has to worry.

9
HENS IN THE HOUSE

The day the first of our young hens began to lay was a day of great excitement for us. As apparently it was for the startled hen who kicked up a racket for the best part of an hour. The discovery that our very first egg contained no trace of a shell, in no way diminished our sense of achievement. Clearly this particular hen intended to specialise in poached or fried eggs. Never good with fried eggs or patient enough to shell a boiled one without breaking it, my immediate reaction was that maybe we were on to a good thing. The shell-less egg might be as good a commercial proposition as the mythical three legged chicken.

On further reflection, I concluded that there weren't really many commercial possibilities in the shell-less egg, the cost of the extensive packaging that they would need would be prohibitive. Safe transport would be a problem too, especially on the local pot-holed roads. So I consulted the hen book to determine the nature of the problem. Lack of grit or calcium was given as the cause. I needn't have worried though, our second egg which appeared three days later came complete with its own shell. The first naked egg was probably just a temporary malfunction.

The hen book, like the sheep and cattle books was on loan from the agricultural section of the local library. I kept them near the back door in case of emergencies. When you are a beginner in farming, emergencies tend to to be fairly frequent.

The librarian who provided me with the poultry book initially

They're all right, they're free-range — it's the ones cooped up in cages that you need to steer clear of.

misunderstood my request. His eyes lit up as he brought me dozens of slim volumes and began to deliver a lecture on the merits of each one. I was loath to stop his highly interesting dissertation, even when it became clear that he thought I had asked for a book on poetry. I hope his obvious disappointment when I corrected him does not reflect the level of literary interest among farmers.

Most of the work with hens involves inventing different ways of keeping them out of the vegetable plot and vunerable parts of the garden. They have a preference for a freshly dug piece of ground where you have just sown a few seeds or planted out some greens. I tried making a gigantic run for them but no matter how high I made the wire there were always a few hens brave enough to fly over the top. I read in the book that if you clipped a little piece off their wings they wouldn't be able to fly so high. It didn't work. Probably because I was always very tentative about this unpleasant task and was constantly afraid of cutting off too much. Clipping their wings took much more out of me than the hens and anyway if they protested too much I usually let them go. Although the operation was said to be painless, the squawking of our hens suggested otherwise.

It's nice to have hens about the place. They scratch contentedly around the yard and garden and the clucking sound they make is pleasant and relaxing. And you soon get used to the male's cock-a-doodle-do at daybreak and simply sleep through it. Anyway, contrary to the popular perception of cocks, some of the ones we've had over the years have been very late risers indeed.

They don't need much to live on, scraps from the house or a few fistfuls of grain will suffice. In return they provide us with fresh eggs, announcing the production of each one with triumphant explosions of sound. The taste of the eggs which we gratefully collect from the wooden egg boxes in the hen house, bear no comparison to their supermarket counterparts. You can always tell a free range egg by the deep colour of its yolk.

They have a reputation as dirty creatures, their droppings having a strong distinctive odour. But their dung is a valuable source of fertility and each hen provides about six stone of this valuable soil enricher every year. Nevertheless, nobody ever voluntarily cleaned out a hen house.

They are interesting creatures to observe and the ease of their reproductive process is especially impressive. Now and then a hen will go 'broody,' that is she will sit on her eggs to

Actually, we were just trying to boost numbers when you rang –

hatch them out. The success of this operation is of course dependant on her having received the attentions of the cock. Assuming that has happened, then it only takes three weeks for the tiny chicks to hatch out. Many women would envy the speed of this process.

Last month our black hen sat on her eggs for over four weeks and produced no chicks. As she had been with the cock, we assume that our Sergeant Pepper, as he is called, must be lacking in the vital area of fertility. This is a pity as he sports a beautiful multicoloured plumage and can crow in perfect tune. The importance of this latter quality might not have occurred to you, but if you ever hear a cock going slightly flat on the doodle-do you will realise how intensely irritating it can be. You don't have to have been a music teacher for this to grate on your nerves. And there's not a lot you can do about a tone deaf cock apart from taking out his voice box and throwing it into a soup.

The only solution for us was to get another cock. Our new one is almost completely white and not nearly as distinctive looking as Sergeant Pepper. We couldn't select a name for him, all the suggestions were too obvious. We kept the Sergeant of course, so there is a bit of jostling for position in the hen house between them at the moment. Like any master of the house, Sergeant Pepper dislikes competition. However, eventually the two harbingers of the dawn will settle down and accept each other.

All this romancing about hens nearly came to an end recently. Inadvertently leaving the back door open while off seeing the cattle, upon my return I found the two cocks and three hens in the kitchen. Unfortunately the dog was close behind me and on seeing him they flew in a noisy panic into the dining room and jumped on to the table to avoid him. Spread across the table was a threequarters completed two thousand piece jigsaw puzzle which my children had been patiently assembling for the past few weeks. Needless to say, it's in bits. Again.

I managed to shoo them off the table but not to calm them down. The feather-filled racket was dreadful. The dog was barking furiously and all the family, who had come to investigate the din, were each trying different actions and sounds in a vain attempt to drive them back out the door. Then suddenly the new white cock, who had probably come from a quieter and more organised household, could tolerate the commotion no longer. He raised his head, took off, and flew straight through the closed window.

The sound of shattering glass silenced both family and hens. It was a dramatic action, worthy of the most fearless circus performer. And as he looked back at us through the broken glass, we were surprised to see he hadn't even been marked.

Today the hens are scratching on the lawn as usual and the jigsaw has been started again. We are making do with a Sellotaped cardboard window but the man assures me he will be here first thing in the morning. And we have a name for the new cock, very obvious really, – we called him Evil Kenevil.

10
DIY FARMING

There is very little profit in farming these days. All the whingeing and moaning you hear in the media from farmers and their representatives is in fact a genuine cry for help from an industry that is gradually going down the tubes as a means of providing a secure living. Admittedly those you see on your television screens warning of the demise of agriculture are either highly paid officials from farming organisations or 'gentleman farmers' who were fortunate enough to inherit half of Wales. But the truth remains; the average farmer is in trouble and needs an alternative source of income if he is to survive on the land.

Tourism is the fastest growing industry at the moment so it makes sense for farmers to combine their farming with some form of income-generating tourist attraction. The traditional way to do this is to go in for bed and breakfast. All you need is a spare bedroom and a reasonably clean frying pan for conjuring up the full breakfast. You'll get the odd difficult customer looking for ensuite and cable television in the bedroom but most of your customers will get a kick out of roughing it in a farmhouse.

The main difficulty with having guests on the farm is that they won't go when they've had their rashers. They will inevitably decide to have a look around the farm before they leave. So you won't be able to go back to bed to recover from your early morning battle with the over-packaged sausages and the spitting pan. Instead, you will have to accompany your ambling visitors, who, having been well filled with your vitamin free breakfast, are now ready to be filled with the joys of nature.

There is nothing more excruciatingly boring for a farmer than having to listen to cooing townies walking round his farm. Every baa of a lamb or grunt of a pig will send them into an exhuberant chorus of oohs and aahs. They're like *Reader's Digest* readers on speed. Everything will be so wonderful and beautiful that you'll wonder if your are inhabiting the same planet as them. And should one of your animals decide to go to the toilet (a very human response in the circumstances) then the excitement of your city slickers will reach fever pitch.

After the tour your visitors will hang around even longer to point out to you how lucky you are to be living in the country far away from the traffic/pollution/muggers/burglars/drugs and all the other dangers of life that apparently begin and end at city boundaries. Of course they won't mention theatres, cinemas, concert halls, restaurants, bookshops, swimming pools or any of the other amenities of city life that are woefully absent and sorely missed in the country.

If it's raining, you can try telling your guests that it's too wet to walk the farm but as farmers are supposed to like rain, this will rarely put them off. One foolproof way of getting rid of them quickly is to tell them that one of your cows died in the night from a mysterious disease and that your farm is about to be cordoned off. This always works but is not good for the future of your business. Animal diseases are taken a lot more seriously nowadays than they were in the past and none of your visitors you eject in this manner will ever return. Neither will you ever meet anybody who lives within a two mile radius of their congested, polluted and burgled house.

Having an open farm for visitors is the logical extension of a bed and breakfast enterprise. If people want to walk around your farm and coo at the animals then why not have them pay for the privilege? You'd probably need to get a few tame rabbits and maybe even an ostrich to provide a bit of variety for your visitors but once you are set up all you have to do is stand at your gate and take their money. You could even get the wife to sell them tea and buns to bring in a bit extra.

One rather serious drawback of the open or visitor farm is the fact that a large proportion of your visitors will be children. The bulk of these will be spoilt and over-indulged in the way that so-called modern children are. They will have been dragged screaming from the television set by their guilt ridden parents who cannot remember the last time their offspring got any fresh air. These protesting siblings will be bored within seconds of entering the gate of your farm and after throwing a few crisp bags at the hens or sticking an ice-cream cone on the back of a calf, they will want to go home. With a bit of luck the more adventurous of them might get their finger bitten by a broody hen or invoke a gentle head butt from an intemperate ram. (You'd need to make sure that you have insurance for this sort of thing – probably the only thing children actually learn from their endless television watching is the word sue.)

Perhaps it's not all their own fault that they are so easily bored? Having been fed on a daily diet of New York murders and ads for Coke what could they possibly find interesting about a few tame animals in a field quietly eating grass?

Another money making possibility is the Pick your own business. With this gimmick, instead of having to pay people to pick your field of strawberries and then transport it to the supermarket or the jam factory, people come to your farm, pick the fruit for you free of charge and then pay you a price far higher than you would get from any supermarket or factory. All you have to do is weigh what they have picked and charge them accordingly. Of course you'll get nothing for the fruit that your customers eat as they pick or the ones that their children throw at each other but you can pitch your price high enough to take account of this.

Pick your own is probably the easiest of those extra farm enterprises and unlike others it only goes on for the few weeks that the fruit is in season. Unfortunately it only seems to work with fruit and vegetables. Attempts to extend this agricultural DIY concept to other areas of farming have met with failure. My 'milk your own cow' afternoon seemed a great idea at the time and there was a fair scattering of takers. My most docile cow, Matilda, was all cleaned up for the day and was the first brought into the yard to stand beside the wooden milking stool and the new shiny bucket. The first milker had dressed himself up as a lion tamer for the occasion. (I later learnt that he was the local accountant.) He moved towards Matilda like a Spanish matador approaching a ferocious bull. As he gingerly edged himself on to the stool Matilda remained calm and relaxed. The lion tamer commenced his first tentative attempts at squeezing her udder to extract the milk. As usual, this was about as successful as a beginner trying to get his first note from a saxophone. The lion tamer tried again but this time Matilda suddenly sniffed the air and, without warning, sprinted out of the yard and way off down the lane leaving him dusting his cowboy suit and looking ridiculous. That was the beginning and the end of my 'milk your own' day.

It was only when I went to give the accountant back his two pounds that I realised the reason for Matilda's hurried departure. The accountant was soaked in aftershave. A popular brand which is unfortunately the same brand worn by the local vet – the same vet who had to pare several nasty corns from Matilda's left foot only a few days previously. Small wonder that it only took one whiff of 'Jungle Juice' or whatever it was called to set her off like a rat from a trap.

I made one further attempt to extend the pick your own concept. Having a 'barbecue your own lamb' day seemed such an obvious idea I was surprised that nobody had thought of it before. I put up coloured posters in the nearby town inviting people to 'picnic on your personally selected roast lamb in the meadow where the lamb had frolicked and played'.

The poster went on to explain that they wouldn't have to slaughter and prepare the lamb themselves – this would be done by a qualified butcher. Mint sauce would be supplied free of charge and the village band would play 'Baa Baa Black Sheep' and other appropriate sheep music to set the mood for the afternoon. As a further incentive, for a mere fiver customers could have the head of their chosen lamb mounted on a genuine oak base to take home with them. This they could place on their mantelpiece or bedside locker to invoke sweet memories of their happy pastoral afternoon.

The weather was perfect on the day and I was encouraged by the fairly large crowd that turned up at the gate. In fact I'd even begun to worry if I'd have enough lambs for them all and might have to call on a few old ewes to make up the numbers. It looked like I was on to a winner with my latest marketing brainwave.

The fact that all the picnickers arrived at the same time should have made me suspicious. It was only when they started taking out gigantic photos of diseased and distressed farm animals and hanging them on my fence posts that I realised that my entire customer base consisted of the membership of several local branches of a national animal rights organisation. When they started chanting slogans like 'Larry Lamb loves life,' 'Bo Peep was no butcher' and, worst of all, 'Barbecue the farmer – not his lamb,' I retreated like a coward to the safety of my house. You can't reason with people who live on bean sprouts.

Perhaps the idea was doomed to failure even without the intervention of the Save the Whalers. Despite our current sophisticated level of civilisation people do not want to believe that their lamb chops come from those playful little woolly crea-

tures that gambol round the meadows in springtime. Or that their morning rasher was once attached to a happy and snortling pink pig. While on the one hand consumers want to know exactly what they are eating, they look to us farmers to protect them from precisely such information.

Of course I had to pay the butcher and the musicians for the afternoon even though neither of them had done any slaughtering or playing. But what annoyed me most about the afternoon was the timely arrival of the local chip van owner who came to feed the hungry protestors. They had built up such an appetite from the provocative and tuneless chanting that he almost ran out of grease. The fact that the chippie in question buys all his potatoes from me in no way lessened my sense of betrayal and moral outrage.

I still have a few less ambitious plans for enlarging my farm income. Zebra farming, cow riding and dung boxing are just a few of them. Writing this book was my latest one.

11
HOLIDAYS

People who live in the country still believe in hard work. The farmer who gets up at six in the morning is proud of himself. For him, hard work is a virtue. It's the reason he was put on this planet. The rest of the world may be getting paid for spending a few hours sitting on a chair. But in farming, the chairs are few and the hours plentiful. The measure of a good farmer is the amount of hours he spends working on his farm. Efficiency studies and productivity assessments belong in the far away world of skyscrapers and computers.

Holiday is not a word in the farmer's vocabulary. Except in its old sense where it means an extra trip to the church on a weekday. Anyway, on such holydays the farmer usually has to get up even earlier to feed the stock before getting into his suit. In farming, holidays interfere with the natural rhythm of the working day. After all, animals and plants never take a day off.

If you work on the land, and can persuade yourself that you need a break, London is a great place to take a holiday. There can be no greater contrast for a farmer than stepping out of his lonely green fields into this vast cosmopolitan city of ten million souls. In fact there is so little green there that it's doubtful that you could graze even one small mountain ewe per square mile.

London is not a place where you are likely to meet many farmers. You'll meet everything else there, men with hair down to their knees, women with none at all and youngsters with all sorts of metal objects stuck on their face, nose, ears and God knows where else. But you'll catch no sight of any of those hard working individuals in muddy boots and carrying EU grant forms that you regularly meet on country roads.

But it's good to get away from the dung heap for a while. And you will be amazed how clean your hands become after only a few days. What's more, you can wear your Sunday clothes on a weekday without the neighbours telling you you're getting a little bit ahead of yourself. In fact to be able to walk down a street and be ignored by everybody is a pleasure you'll never experience in the country.

Of course for country people, cities can be frightening places. All those moving staircases can be difficult to manipulate if you are used to doing your walking in grassy fields. Picking the exact moment to jump off these elevators is a skill that the average farmer seldom gets a chance to learn. As a result, I'm sure many a farmer visiting London has lost more than one pair of boots to these unstoppable electric stairways.

Doors that open all by themselves can be unnerving too.

You were the one who wanted a working farm holiday – how was I to know this one was a sewage farm?

How do they work? And more importantly, how can you be sure they won't decide to close just as you are going in? Especially those big thick ones they have on the tube. I've never heard of anybody being squashed by these doors. But then the owners of the London underground are not likely to advertise those sort of statistics, are they?

Having just had a holiday in Her Majesty's capital, I can offer sound advice to any organic farmer planning to take a break there. If you are at any social gathering in London and somebody asks you what you do, on no account admit to being an organic farmer. Tell them you are a tax inspector, deep sea diver, or even a ballet dancer. Tell them you're a body washer in the local morgue. Tell them anything. But don't mention the word organic.

Just about everybody in London has read that article about organic farmers. You know the one where it said that organic farmers have the highest sperm count. And that everybody else's ability to replace themselves is diminishing. So as soon as you admit to your chosen vocation you start to get funny looks. And not just from the women.

One very attractive young woman spent an entire evening telling me how in thirty years time the only people capable of reproducing the human species would be organic farmers! The significance of this would be far reaching. In a world consisting entirely of farmers, who would post out our EU payments? Of course, on the positive side, there would be nobody to tax our hard earned few pounds. Or destroy our markets by suggesting that our animals were mad.

This well-read woman had a lovely accent and if only I had not had to catch the last bus to Camden I might have listened longer. Anyway most organic farmers have already done a pretty good job of reproducing themselves. And after another thirty years of hard work on the land which of us would be either willing or able?

Two Highly Commendeds for chickweed and a Best in Show for his blackfly!

17
STUDENT POWER

Sooner or later things go wrong in farming. It's even happened with pages 32 and 44 of this book which are in the wrong order. **Sorry!**

Those, like farmers, who are their own boss and who spend their working lives at home, inevitably attract the envy of friends and acquaintances in so-called regular jobs. People who work for themselves are seen as free spirits who can work when and how they like; or not at all if it doesn't suit them. They can take a holiday or spend a day in town at the drop of a hat. The self-employed answer to nobody.

The truth is rather different. Although in theory you can take a day off whenever you like, in reality it takes at least a funeral before you do. And the deceased would have to be somebody fairly close. You can't become ill either. There is little point in ringing up the sheep house to say you won't be in for a few days. The sheep aren't going to jump out of their pens and collect their own hay from the hay shed. And, if you are a vegetable grower, unless you have some contagious disease that can be readily transmitted when handling the vegetables, your supermarket customers will have little understanding if you fail to deliver.

Fortunately there are numerous foreign students who want to work on farms and experience a rural lifestyle. Mainly from Germany but also from further afield, some are students of agriculture who are interested in gaining first hand practical experience, others merely want to spend time in the countryside and improve their English. A few, of course, are chancers who want a free holiday. The trick is to weed out the unsuitables in advance.

Many students who write expressing the desire to reduce the summer workload have no idea what working on a farm is like. And coming from more densely populated countries they have little notion either of how isolated country life can be. That the nearest disco might be a twenty-mile cycle away seldom occurs to them. But you get better at analysing their letters and recognising the dreamers who see farming as some spiritually profound

'I thought you said punk was old hat anyway -'

have no place on it either. If you have a shed that's well away from the route of the walk then you should hide all your sickly animals there for the afternoon. It must be well out of earshot of your visitors. When your guests are being suitably complimentary about the health of your stock in the fields the last thing you need is a sorrowful 'moo' or 'baa' blowing in the wind and some astute farmer, who only came because he expected your farm to be a mess, to say 'Can we take a look at what you have in the shed?'

It would be better to get your animal failures off the farm altogether for the day. It might be easy enough to find a nearby farmer who would be prepared to hide all your hospital cases behind his hayshed during the walk, but it would be asking the impossible to expect him to be able to keep his mouth shut about it. The temptation to ruin your agricultural graduation would be too great for even the most kindly of your neighbours. So if you haven't got a suitably remote shed on your farm then probably the best thing to do is to get up early in the morning before the first of your neighbours and quietly shoo the unwanted animals on to the road. As they are unhealthy they won't go too far and you can pick them up again after dark. Naturally this course of action is not open to you if you live on a busy main road.

When showing off your poultry flock don't worry too much about the state of the hen house. If you have time to clean it out well and good but as the management of the poultry flock is traditionally the responsibility of women and children, a filthy hen house will not reflect badly on yourself. What is important is that the farm walkers see a plentiful supply of eggs. It's no good saying you collected ten dozen this morning before everybody arrived. Seeing is believing with sceptical farmers so you need to leave the eggs there for all to view.

Of course your hundred and twenty hens will never lay ten

AUTUMN IN THE NEW FOREST

dozen eggs on the one day so you will need to leave some of the previous day's bounty in the nest boxes as well to make up the numbers. But be careful not to leave more eggs in the boxes than you have hens. There might be some pedantic farmer on the walk who is prepared to go to the bother of counting them just for the pleasure of putting one over on you. And if you have to buy eggs, make sure you place them in the nesting boxes with the date stamp downwards. Farmers who have never had their farms walked can be very spiteful when visiting the farms of those more favoured.

If your vegetable field is not looking its best with thistles and docks towering over your stunted seedlings, the obvious solution is to get down on your hands and knees and tidy it up. Alternatively you can tell your visitors that your vegetables are grown organically. People expect to see weeds in an organic field. Indeed they would be very suspicious if there were none. You can be sure that no matter how big a mess your vegetable field is in, most of the non-farmers on the walk, will commend your decision to go organic and save the environment. The organic explanation will also save you any embarrassment you might suffer if your cabbages are covered with caterpillars or your lettuce is teeming with greenfly. Nobody expects organic produce to look good. The point about organic vegetables is that they are good for us. In fact to the committed organic consumer if the pests won't eat your vegetables then they can't be safe for humans. So in your organic field the rougher everything looks the better. Just ensure that all your fertiliser bags and sprays are safely out of sight.

There are three distinct types of people who attend farm walks. The smallest, but the most vital group if your walk is to be a success, are those who genuinely come to observe your farming system and to learn from it. They are experienced and perpetual farm walkers who never seem to learn enough about farming. These serious individuals can be relied on to ask all the right questions thus allowing you to boast unashamedly about your agricultural skills. A few of them will even bring note books. This lends a certain gravitas to the day and helps to keep the less serious visitors in line.

A larger group are those whose only purpose in walking your farm is to find fault with it. Standing at the back of the crowd as you answer questions on your lambing percentages or on the composition of your cattle feed, they will mutter and snigger at your every word like unruly children in a classroom. As you speak they will be examining a loosely hung gate that

needs attention or shaking a piece of fencing that is in danger of falling. In the vegetable field they will squeeze the heart of your smallest cabbage and shake their heads sadly. Or taste a strawberry only to spit it out with a startled cry of pain. In the cattle field they will carefully turn over a dung pat with their sticks and then frown in harmony to create the impression that they have found evidence of mad cow disease or worse in your cattle droppings.

But by far the largest section of any farm walk will be those naturally curious country folk who have come to see how you live. They have no interest in sniffing your hay or feeling the weight of your turnips. They want to see the inside of your house so that they can confirm their speculations as to your lifestyle. For them the obligatory tea and buns in your kitchen at the end of the walk with perhaps even the possibility of a trip upstairs to your bathroom is their reward for trudging round your fields for the afternoon. On their minds as the time for tea draws nearer will be important questions like what kind of cooker do you have? And is your kitchen table made of real oak or only a cheap imitation? Will they find ordinary soap in the bathroom or are you one of these uppity people who uses shower gel? Do you eat ordinary fare or will your kitchen be full of fancy foods such as exotic pastas, garlic bread and dried French champignons? Not all the questions in their minds will be as seemingly harmless as those. Some will be hoping to find a bin full of empty whisky bottles confirming their suspicions that you are a secret drinker. Or a letter on the kitchen table from the Retired Convicts' Association showing that you were not always the law-abiding citizen that you now appear to be.

The quality of the tea and buns will also come under close scrutiny from this same group. With the buns, a balance needs to be struck between the basic and very familiar 'rock bun' that adorns the table at all rural events and the more sophisticated and grandiose 'fairy cake' of the up-market dinner party. If your buns are too elaborate you will be seen as trying to show off. Yet if they are too simple and lacking even a few currants, you will be viewed as mean.

Given that any part of your house to which the terminally curious gain access will be examined in detail for any scrap of private information, it's best to remove any item that might give them cause to gossip about you at their next social occasion. Everything relating to your income such as bank statements, tax demands or subsidy cheques should be safely locked away. Farmers will stoop to any depths to find out how much another farmer earns. Hard information about a neighbour's income will pass many a long evening in the local pub. And there is a very real danger that any such free flowing information will become enlarged and exaggerated before finding its way into the offices of the local tax inspector.

Don't be tempted to leave any of your extensive range of farming books lying casually around the kitchen. A weighty and well thumbed agricultural tome lying open on the chair beside the cooker might seem like an obvious way to impress upon your guests the immense range and depth of your agricultural

knowledge. But 'book farmers' are frowned upon by 'native farmers'. Good farmers are produced by breeding and sweat, not by poring over books written by people who, if they were minding their farms properly, would not have the time to be indoors with pen and paper. Anyway, since farmers are being constantly harassed by wads of impossible forms from the E.U. they have developed a distinct aversion to anything on paper.

If your family have been leafing through holiday brochures or the travel sections of the Sunday newspapers, make sure the evidence is safely hidden from your guests. A truly hard working farmer never has time for a holiday. Neither does he ever make sufficient money to be able to afford one. It is the lot of the farmer, regardless of how good prices and grants might be, to have a level of income consistent only with 'merely surviving' or 'just getting by'. Maintaining an image of abject poverty is an unwritten oath of farming. Its universal maintenance is as vital to the practice of farming as the Hippocratic Oath is to medicine. To give the impression that your financial situation is any better than your farming neighbours who work every hour God sends for a less than adequate minimum wage, will provoke a level of hostility and envy that will render it difficult for you and yours to remain farming in the same neighbourhood.

If your children are at that difficult teenage state where their hair is long and dirty and they look (hopefully wrongly) like regular drug abusers, it might be best to slip them a fiver and send them off to the pictures for the afternoon. For traditional country folk, long hair and a general scruffy appearance invokes wild and highly judgmental images of hippies, tree-huggers and even Save the Whalers. A lengthy mane stands for anti-foxhunting, vegetarianism, freedom of movement for rats, human rights for insects and anything else that can make life difficult for the traditional farmer. Not to mention the lack of discipline that an untidy head symbolises. (Farmers are big on discipline). Of course if your own hair is long you will presumably have the good sense to tie it up for the afternoon.

Assuming you manage to avoid the more obvious pitfalls of opening your gates to public scrutiny and succeed in getting all the hangers-on out of your kitchen before dark without offence, then you can justifiably view your farm walk as a success and take your rightful place among the nation's farmers. Give yourself the evening off to bask in the glow of acceptance. All the muck from those inquisitive boots that found their way into your bedroom can be cleaned up in the morning.

13
CONVERSING WITH COWS

Those like farmers and lighthouse keepers who spend a lot of time working on their own, generally form the habit of talking to themselves. While one-way conversations are viewed as a sign of insanity or at least a serious mental weakness by those who live and work surrounded by people, the opposite is the case. Talking to oneself has many advantages over talking to others. In a world of individualism where everybody is imbued with the need to express their own point of view, we rarely get an opportunity to speak for very long without being contradicted. To lecture at length on the state of the world or the meaning of existence without fear of being interrupted is an experience that's generally given only to clergymen, nagging wives, and short-tempered teachers. The rest of us have to talk to ourselves.

The farmer has a double advantage. Not only can he converse with himself for hours on end in the solitude of his fields, but he also has a ready made non-critical audience on hand if he needs it. Assuming his fences are secure, in his animals he has a captive assembly.

Of course, not all animals are good lis-

Just ignore him - he always starts fancying his chances as we get towards the County Show!

teners. Young animals are generally the worst. Small lambs or calves will, like children, generally scamper off down the field in the middle of your most important sentence leaving you wondering if they were paying attention to anything at all. But at least with animals this doesn't start you worrying about their future educational prospects. Not being the parent their schooling need not concern you.

Hens are the most inattentive. Not only will they not stay still while you speak, they will completely ignore you and continue scratching and cackling away to themselves as if you weren't there. Even reciting your grandmother's favourite recipe for chicken soup will not attract their interest. Turkeys are no better. And they will look at you through their startled eyes as if they consider the content of your dissertation to be completely preposterous. One would think that a rather obvious way of attracting their attention would be to open your lecture with the singing of a popular Christmas carol, but even this has no effect. Clearly the English language, even when spoken at its finest or sung, is way beyond their limited intellectual capabilities.

Horses are pretty good listeners. They have all the qualities of a fascinated audience remaining still, quiet and intent as your impressive intellectualism is shared with them. However they have one disadvantage as listeners, most of them are too tall. The successful speaker needs to be able to talk down to his audience. Knowledge is always dispensed from on high. This is not possible with horses. Because of their height, you get a crick in your neck talking up to them. It's completely impossible to feel superior while speaking below the level of your listener's teeth. Your belief in the validity of your arguments seems to dissipate with the constant stretching of your neck. That's why Napoleon always stood on a banana box.

Cows are the best audience. Standing or sitting they absorb your ideas from below with the calm of the converted. They remain impassive for hours, eager to devour each and every vocal jewel regardless of quantity. Like all good listeners they punctuate your diatribe with a slight flick of the tail or with an occasional knowing shake of the head. Regardless of the difficulty of the topic or the frequent use of specialist words, they remain composed and collected. No matter how controversial the subject they are too well mannered to show their irritation by frowning, tut-tutting or shaking their heads in disbelief. Sometimes their attention is distracted by an urgent call of nature. In that they are no different from their human counterparts. But unlike humans they don't have to put the speaker off his stride by making a noisy exit from the lecture hall. When addressing an audience of cows, no interval is required.

A further advantage of talking to cows is the lack of any language barrier. The German and French breeds remain as attentive as the English. And the English speaking cows are not in any way deterred if your presentation is overly pregnant with quotes in the vernacular from foreign sources. Obviously there were no cows around when the tower of Babel was erected.

In the past the great thinkers went off to live in caves remaining silent for forty years. Like cows, they ate, slept and thought. But in the noisy modern world that we inhabit today, we seldom associate silence with wisdom or passivity with intellectual confidence. Thus, the cow's intelligence is never recognised. Quiet confident individuals who verbalise

very infrequently are wrongly considered to be 'bovine'. Those concerned with animal rights or political correctness would do well to seek to correct this injustice.

In a world where lonely hearts columns have even invaded some of the quality Sunday newspapers and counselling is our major growth industry, those many thousands of individuals who constantly seek a sympathetic and non judgemental listening ear might do well to consider going outside the normal human sources of understanding. Ask the next lonely livestock farmer you see talking to himself. He'll be quick to tell you that without the company of his animals his very sanity would be at stake.

14
RURAL LIBERALS

A neighbour of mine had to get the vet last week. He hates the vet. But then he hates anyone who earns more than himself. Being a farmer, for him that means almost everybody.

My neighbour is not the most super-efficient or modern farmer. His idea of a gate is a few gorse bushes held together with a couple of strands of blue binder twine. Nothing terribly

That's right, we're the new people who've moved into the cottage – twelve years ago.

wrong with that of course. But he could at least replace the bushes every few years. If only for the sake of keeping his sheep out of nearby gardens.

The same man makes much of the fact that he was farming organically long before the notion ever came to the attention of the trendies.. But of course the real reason for the environomental purity of his farm is the fact that he was always too mean to buy fertiliser and sprays for his land or antibiotics for his animals. In common with a number of ageing farmers in the country, he was organic by default rather than commitment.

Anyway, he had to call the vet for an old grey faced ewe who was heavily in lamb. He described the symptoms of the problem to me in great detail but I'll spare you the particulars of the ewe's distress in case you're having your plate of pasta at the moment.

When he had convinced himself that he had no option but to spend money on the vet, he went off to the phone box in the village to ring. He's not a frequent user of the phone. So when he was unable to locate the slot for his coins, he assumed the money box was stolen and called to the local post office to report the theft. There, the helpful postmistress introduced him to the latest technological swindle, the call card.

The local postmistress is one strong lady. Very little has ever escaped her attention. But nothing could have prepared her for the reaction of my neighbour when asked for £2.00 for the call card. 'Did she think he wanted a vet from Australia? Fearing for the heart of the old man, she allowed him to use her own

'You the wind-farmer? Some of your
wind's got out into my garden and
it's playing merry hell with my
prize runners -'

phone. At a small profit.

So it was a highly agitated shepherd that waited the arrival
of the vet. In fact he was so stressed that his wife had to leave
the dishes to make him a second pot of tea. Before he could
finish it, a car came down the lane carrying his second shock of
the day.

Inside the car was the vet. With long hair and eye shadow. A
woman. The vet was a woman! Or as my neighbour more
colourfully described her, 'a fine strapping painted lady. Didn't
even look like a vet. A fancy lady in a fancy car. Good thing I
wasn't getting her to sort out a bull. Can she not get herself a
husband ?'

Actually he said much more than that. He tends to get his
prejudice against women mixed up with other social issues.
Like gay rights, women priests, and the ewe premium. And he
has an awful lot to say on the subject of hippies. Or 'them long
haired environmental types' as he prefers to call them. Socially
and politically he is somewhere to the right of Attila the Hun.

The old ewe is better now. She gave birth to twins last
week. But the nature of her gynaecological difficulties will
never be known. 'How could I ask a woman about things like
that?' said my neighbour when asked. 'You can't talk about
such things in mixed company.' There seemed little point in
suggesting to him that a female vet might have a better understanding of these things than most.

Now readers in cities and liberal country towns may well
think my neighbour is a far from typical example of the rural
male. They probably believe that the liberation of women and
the equality of the sexes was completed a long time ago.
Sometime before the introduction of the microwave. Hours of
listening to Radio 4 and watching various pony tailed intellec-
tuals on the TV might have given them the notion that they are
now living in some kind of new and modern society. Such people need to spend some time
in the more isolated parts of
the country.

For this man, country
women have only two important functions. The same ones
they have had since the time
of Adam's mother. Children
and tea. They exist to produce both. Not in the same
quantities of course! But they
do have a lot more freedom
than previous generations.
After all, there was no such
thing as tea bags in their
grandparent's time. Or electric kettles.

'Happens every year - soon
after Christmas he stomps
up here with an armful
of hideous ties !'

15
FEMALE FARMERS

Country people are renowned for calling a spade a spade. They don't hold much store by all these fancy words that have come into our language as a result of the new politically correct language police. A 'traveller' to them still means somebody who is going on a journey. A 'partner' is somebody you go into business with or what cowboys call their friends. And you never hear a thirsty farmer in his local shouting for the 'barperson'.

Nevertheless, I was very surprised at a photograph in a national farming newspaper a few weeks ago. It was a photo of a young woman. The woman was all dressed up and smiling from the seat of a high powered tractor. She was demonstrating the merits of this new fancy piece of machinery at an agricultural show. Women are used for selling everything these days, even to farmers, so there's nothing surprising about that.

But what did surprise me was the caption that accompanied the photograph of this female farmer. The respected newspaper described her occupation, not as a farmer but as a 'farmerette'. Now when we use 'ette' in the English language it is generally taken to mean a smaller version of the real thing. A kitchenette is a small kitchen. So the implication is very clear. A female farmer is somehow less than her male counterparts. A farmerette is the agricultural equivalent of 'the little woman'.

Farming is one of the few areas which seems to have escaped the attention of the women's movement. Most male farmers

Which way to the centre of the village?
This <u>is</u> the centre of the village!

are married so there are plenty of farmers' wives. Traditionally they mind the house, keep a few chickens and bottle feed the weak calves and lambs. But the full time female farmer has yet to establish her rightful place in the modern world.

Perhaps it's the fact that the word farmerette sounds so much like launderette that makes it seem so offensive. Although I'm sure there is some smart lad married to a female farmer who's thinking at this very moment that the only difference between a launderette and a farmerette is the fact that you have to bring your clothes yourself to a launderette to get them washed. But then there are some types we'll never put manners on.

The livestock mart is a place where the maleness of farming is readily demonstrated. The only women you will see there will be working in the canteen frying up the hearty breakfasts for the men. The sales ring will be as masculine as a monastery. Presumably women farmers have to get a man to do their buying and selling for them?

I wonder who thought up the word 'farmerette?' You never hear a female doctor being called a doctorette. Or a female cook being called a chefette. Indeed if you follow this misuse of language to its logical conclusion then a father should be called a motherette. A son could be a daughterette. And what would be the female equivalent of a cigarette? I suppose we'd have to call it a fagette?

16
CHICKEN OR EGG?

My mother-in-law never tires of telling the story of the farm labourer who, when asked how he liked his egg, replied 'with another'. Anyone who gets up early in the morning and puts on the kettle before going expectantly to the hen house in search of breakfast will empathise with this frequently quoted farm labourer. Finding one solitary egg or even less in a crowded hen house can seriously dampen one's spirits for the rest of the day.

There'll probably be half a dozen hens sitting on nothing so if you are prepared to wait a few hours you might be able to have your eggs later on. But there are no certainties with egg laying. Many hens like to sit in the egg boxes just for the hell of it.

It might seem like a simple matter to nip down to the local shop and buy yourself half a dozen brown specimens to tide you over but this option is not open to any self respecting poultry farmer. Better to go hungry than make such a public admission of defeat. And you can do without the helpful tips you'll get about feeding hens, the advantages of selective breeding and those boring stories about champion egg layers.

Of course you could drive to a shop where nobody knows you. But as country people make it their business to know everybody within a seemingly impossible physical radius, you would have to drive a long distance for your egg. Even then you could never be certain that yet another farming failure was not noticed by someone. Perhaps it's because very little ever happens in the country that very little is ever missed.

Even worse than finding no egg in the hen house is finding a hen sitting on a dozen and refusing to get off them. Any attempt to extract a pair for yourself would be met with a sharp pecking of your invading fingers. Anyway, you can never be certain how long the hen has been sitting on the eggs. Even a bowl of nut-filled muesli with added roughage can appear more appetising when compared with the prospect of cracking open

You and your ruddy home improvements!

an egg that might have started on its way to being a chicken.

But of course the whole purpose of eggs in the first place is not the making of Pavlova but to produce chickens. And fluffy chickens pecking their way round the yard is a joy to behold. The trouble is that most chickens will grow up to be cocks and all except those those very new to farming will be aware that cocks don't lay eggs. All cocks ever do is wake you up in the morning and eat your expensive grain. A more non productive farm animal is difficult to imagine.

As with most problems the simple solution is to do nothing for the moment. But as the cocks get bigger and eat more, you will eventually reach the point where the cost of your hen food is far greater than the value of eggs produced, no matter how highly you price your eggs. Something has to be done about the cocks. It might take the fact that more chicks are on the way to spur you into action, but action cannot be postponed for ever.

The obvious solution is to gather up the cocks in the hen-house as they sleep, chop their heads off with a sharp axe and throw them into a pot. In one fowl swoop your problem is solved. There are two main difficulties with this deceptively simple solution. The lesser of the two is the fact there is very little meat on a cock from an egg laying breed of hens. They are hardly worth the effort of cooking. If you have any sort of appetite at all you'd need at least half a dozen to make a decent meal. Furthermore, the meat is inclined to be rather tough.

The second and more serious problem is the difficulty, physical and moral, of sneaking up on the poor defenceless birds in the dark of night and chopping their heads off. After all, these are the little babies you doted on as they cuddled under their proud mother's feathers and chirped contentedly in the spring sunshine. Anyway how can you hold a bird down with one hand and chop his head off with the other? You run the risk of missing the spot and taking your whole arm off.

Culling cocks is an activity that requires considerable advance thought and preparation. But don't expect any helpful advice or offers of assistance from family and friends. In fact if you are in any way unsure of yourself in matters of murdering animals, it's better not to mention your plans to them at all.

A SPRINKLING OF VISITORS . . .

They certainly won't offer to help and their high moral arguments and expressions of horror will only postpone the deed for another few months and have you even deeper in debt to your local grain merchant.

After the deed you will have many thoughts of the chicken and egg variety. The meaning and purpose of life will weigh heavily on your mind. Vegetarianism as an option will be considered again. And you will have learnt that the amount of meat on a cockerel is really surprisingly small.

12
THE FARM WALK

You haven't really arrived as a farmer until you are asked to host a farm walk. This is a sort of agricultural open day when all in sundry are invited to your farm to walk your fields and see how good a farmer you are. For a new farmer it's a kind of 'coming out,' an opportunity to present your new successful lifestyle to the world.

To be asked to host a farm walk is to be offered a level of rural recognition that cannot be refused, no more than a third division soccer player can turn down a chance to play in the premier league. But it's an event that's fraught with many dangers, the chief one being that you might end up as the laughing stock of the entire neighbourhood and beyond. So to ensure its success there are a few preparations that need to be undertaken in advance of the big day. You can't let down those who had sufficient confidence in your farming methods to request the walk, by shamefully

parading your failures for all to see.

Most of those who come to farm walks expect to see healthy animals grazing lush green fields. So it's important that you don't disappoint them. The thin heifer that nearly died of pneumonia last winter or the dirty ewe whose wool has been half eaten by maggots have no place on the route of the planned walk. Three legged lambs or calves with stiff necks

Steady, Shep, steady –

and natural process that requires little intervention on the part of man. Those who have seen too many paintings of brightly dressed peasants dancing in the hay fields. Or have watched too many advertisements that show bronzed young models delicately sipping vodka in the middle of a field of flowing corn.

So when an engineering student from Rome writes to tell you that he is consumed with a desire to 'commune with nature', or an ecology student in Berlin cites the fact that she has a pet rabbit as evidence of experience of working with animals, you can be fairly certain they won't fit in with farm or family. Nevertheless, despite the screening process, disasters can occur.

Once, when I drove to the village to pick up a Spanish student it became immediately apparent that I had made a serious mistake. Dressed in an immaculately pressed three piece suit with matching tie, he descended from the bus like a jetsetter who had just alighted from Concorde. And the three large cases he was struggling to carry suggested he had come equipped with more than one such suit. However I brought him home and made him welcome. When I showed him round the farm and it became clear that he was more interested in preserving the flawless state of his clothes than he was in my animals, I had a feeling his stay would be brief. But I was still surprised to find him gone the next morning. He left a note pinned to the kitchen door. It read 'Nice people you are but the life here is very hard. Sorrie'. I still wonder how he managed to carry all that luggage by himself. Perhaps I misjudged his aptitude for heavy farm work?

Another time a large German girl arrived. As I carried her battered guitar inside I was struck by the unholy thought that she looked like someone who could plough a field without the aid of a tractor or any other mechanical device. When it emerged that she was a refugee from another farming family and had left them hurriedly as a result of some vague and minor misunderstanding, I suspected there might be problems. Later, when I showed her to her room and she asked me to take out the bed as she preferred to sleep on the floor, I was even more certain that there were a few cultural differences that might not be too easy to overcome. Sure enough, she was another early morning absconder. Her morning note, stuck to a jar of raspberry jam in this instance, stated that we were 'too materialistic and conventional' for her liking. Although I resolved there and then to begin a collection of these early

I told you not to criticise his ploughing!

morning notes, I'm happy to say I haven't had any more since.

It's not surprising that the arrival of a student can cause difficulties for a family. When we consider how difficult it can be, at times, to get on with those people we know and have chosen to live with, small wonder then, that the introduction of a complete stranger into your household can often be a traumatic event for all concerned. And of course, there is the effect they can have on your animals to consider. There are some whose mere presence in the yard can induce dramatic panic attacks in previously peaceful hens and set them off flying and screeching to all points of the compass. There are others who only have to put one foot in the meadow to set your horse cantering away at great speed to the next county. Such students are generally better employed in the vegetable field. However, commercial horticulture can present its own set of problems to the uninitiated. Students who cannot tell the difference between a valuable crop of early french beans and the weeds that grow beside them or who are unable to walk the perfectly straight lines that separate the rows of lettuce, might have to content themselves with the internationally unpopular task of cleaning out the calf house.

If everything fails, they can always be left to help in the house. Standards of cleanliness are apparently much higher in other European countries so, if willing, foreign students will find many areas that they will wrongly believe haven't been cleaned for years. Some of them may volunteer to help with the cooking. But a word of caution might be advisable here. It's not that easy to do a heavy day's work on a diet of heavily vinegared lettuce and a plate of bean sprouts.

So while in general student workers are a bit like the national soccer team, either a great success or a total disaster, the following collection of hints drawn from my many years of experience in international relations might help other farmers to avoid some of the more obvious pitfalls. A small amount of careful preparation in advance of the student worker's arrival can save you weeks of seething frustration and discomfort in your own home.

Things to do before the student worker arrives

The first thing is to find a large sheet of foolscap paper and a brightly coloured crayon or marker. (A stock marker would be ideal). On the sheet of paper, in large letters, write your name. Now affix the paper securely to your favourite chair. (or to all your chairs if you like). By this simple action you will avoid being banished to the coldest corner of the room, by all but the most illiterate of students. I use organic spring onion tape for the sticking operation. Not only does it add a touch of authenticity to your green household, but as it is very long you will have plenty left over for sticking your name on the stereo, or drinks cabinet, or any other coveted possession you may wish to protect.

If you intend to give your student a bed to sleep in, then it's vital to remove the mattress before they arrive. This will reduce the danger of them oversleeping in the morning. (This is a heavy job, I know, but it's not really one you can get the student to do.) Dragging a heavy mattress to an outside shed and hiding it under a few bales of straw may seem like a lot of trouble. But you can be certain the effort will be repaid in the number of extra hours of work that will be extracted from the student as a result.

It's a good idea also to thoroughly check the door of their room. Open and close it a few times. If it squeaks, then you will need to apply a small drop of oil to its hinges. After applying the oil, check that it now opens and closes quietly. Its worth taking trouble over this. There is nothing worse than being woken up early in the morning by the sound of a squeaky door, especially if you have a musical ear. This simple tip enables any student, except the most heavily built, to get up quietly without disturbing your sleep.

Next, examine all the light bulbs in the house, preferably after dark. Take out any you don't really need. Replace all the others with bulbs that have a low wattage. Most students come from energy-rich countries where lights are left on all the time so this handy hint will save you pounds. However, a word of warning may be necessary here. Be careful not to overdo this process. Otherwise, you may be woken some dark morning by the noise of the student falling over the furniture. Not to mention the danger to yourself and your family.

If you are technically competent in electrical matters, then it will be well worth your while turning down the thermostat on your immersion heater. Students are notorious for having baths and showers, even the ones that never get themselves dirty. If the temperature on the thermostat is turned down low enough, it will have a dramatic effect on the frequency of the student's bathing. (You can always boil a kettle for yourself.)

Finally it's important to prepare yourself for the many questions the student will ask upon their arrival. The most common of these is likely to concern Saturdays. I've never been able to improve on the approach of a well known local poultry farmer, a man highly experienced in these matters. When asked by students if they have to work on Saturdays, his standard reply is " Well, tell me now, do you have to eat on Saturdays?"

18
SUMMER HAYZE

Watching your neighbours is an essential part of farming. If the farmer next door starts his ploughing early then all the others will reconsider their view that it's not dry enough yet to start. If one farmer delays sowing his corn, then those who have already sown theirs will worry that

CAUTION
—
FARMER
IN CAR
AHEAD
STARING
AT STATE
OF THE
FIELDS

maybe he knows something about the weather that they don't. There are a few independent farmers who do their own thing regardless of what the others are doing. But these confident types only serve to make farming life even more confusing than it already is for the rest of us.

Perhaps the biggest gamble in the farming calender is making hay. No other activity better reflects the differing characters of those who tend the land. It is the hay making process that separates the optimist from the pessimist, the gambler from the cautious, and the confident from the not so certain.

Making hay is a risky business. Not only do you need at least one full week of dry, sunny weather, you need to be able to predict when it is coming. In recent years the few parts of the country that were fortunate enough to have the sun for a full week in June or July rarely had a second one.

The precise time he decides to mow depends very much on the farmer's particular temperament. A man's character is clearly on display in his hay field. By his attitude to hay making, a farmer shows his attitude to life.

The cautious farmer

The cautious farmer waits until the fine weather is well and truly established before deciding to cut half the field. Rarely is it dry enough before the weather breaks again and this first cut is washed away. Losing half his hay makes him even more cautious so he spends the next few weeks listening to every available

weather forecast on radio and TV as well as
ringing the highly expensive weatherline for
farmers, several times a day. No forecast is
ever certain enough for him as he scours the
wave bands and hounds the met. service for a
promise of fine weather.

By mid August his frustration is com-
pounded by the fact that all his neighbours
have their bales safely in the hay shed and are
taking day trips with their families to the sea-
side. Driven to distraction by the few non
swimming farmers who delight in telling him
that hay will be very dear this year, he suddenly mows the second half of his field without even glancing at the sky. No sooner has
he put the tractor away than the biggest
downpour of the year occurs and he loses the
lot.

The copy cat farmer

The copy cat farmer has a different attitude to
hay making. Paying no attention to weather
predictions, he travels the roads watching his
neighbours. While he might be happy to
ignore the odd maverick farmer cutting away,
as soon as he sees more than three or four
neighbours at work he rushes home and cuts
his own. His reasons for adopting this
approach to saving winter fodder are some-
what contradictory. On the one hand he
argues that so many of his neighbours can't
be wrong. On the other he derives consola-
tion from the fact that if they are wrong and
he loses his hay he won't be the only one in
that unfortunate position. Farming being no
more equitable than life itself, the copy cat
farmer is generally a more successful haymak-
er than his more cautious equivalent.

Born again farmers

A third and rapidly increasing group of hay

ALL IS SAFELY GATHERED IN . . .

makers could best be described as the 'born again' farmers. Driven from gainful employment in the city by a vague and romantic desire to get back to nature, and other similar symptoms of mid-life crises, their knowledge of agriculture is gleaned from a huge collection of glossy books bought in the lifestyle section of upmarket bookshops. That these books are written for the most part by urban refugees like themselves who at least had the good sense to supplement their inevitable farming losses by writing books, never occurs to these converts. Thus, the born again farmer obeys the books and cuts his hayfield just after the protein level in the grass reaches its maximum and just before it begins to go to seed. As pinpointing the exact few hours when this occurs requires such constant vigilance, the born again farmer is left with little time to take account of local conditions, or to consider the advice of the 'born into it' local farmers. Such farmers frequently outbid each other at hay auctions.

Perhaps the most successful producers of winter fodder are the soulless cowards. They don't make hay at all. These farmers consider the risks associated with haymaking to be too great in this unpredictable climate. Not for them the sweet aroma of new mown hay or the shrieks of happy children playing around the bales. Ignoring the inspiration behind millions of lines of poetry, thousands of pieces of music, and an incalculable number of romantic liaisons, these Philistines choose to make silage instead.

Who ever made love in a silage pit ?

Really ?

It happens every year like this !

19
LOOKING AHEAD

Many people spend their lives living in the future. While a certain amount of looking ahead is necessary, those whose business it is to teach us how to live stress-free lives are always encouraging us to live in the present. Why waste our lives worrying about things that may never happen? Good advice this may be - but it is no use to farmers. There will be no crops in the autumn if they are not sown in spring, no lambs for Easter if the farmer forgets to bring the ram to the ewes, and no turkeys for Christmas if the chicks are not ordered early in the summer.

Christmas is the last thing on a farmer's mind during the long hazy days of summer. His stock are happily grazing the lush summer growth and the ears of corn are beginning to fill out. It's the time of year when the farmer is the envy of all those who work indoors. Yet that is precisely the time of the year when turkey producers should be thinking about Christmas. Time to decide how many birds he will raise this year.

There is always a great demand for free range birds and most producers could sell twice as many as they produce. But if the turkeys are genuinely free range – that is, allowed to roam freely wherever they want – then there is a limit to how many can be let loose around the farm. Fifty seems to be the magic number. Any more than that tends to lead to chaos. As well as dirt on every boot and shoe that comes into the kitchen.

Turkeys are generally bought by farmers when they are three or four weeks old. Not being much bigger than your hand at that stage, they seldom stray more than a few yards from their house. In fact in the first few weeks the more reluctant ones may have to be encouraged to leave the safety of their cosy strawfilled quarters. But they soon find their way to the garden and that's when whatever number of them there are always seems to be too many. Successful gardening and free range turkey production are in no way compatible.

It's not just the fact that the turkeys make such a mess of

Nice Bessy -

the barbecue area, although listening to visiting city friends being childish about turkey droppings can be intensely irritating. Especially when the same people are constantly boasting to their neighbours about their specially ordered free range bird. No. What's annoying about the turkeys is their taste in shrubs. Ignoring all the less attractive specimens, they always head straight for the clematis. It's usually just one bird who discovers the tender shrub draped over the old tree stump. But she is soon joined by the others who, over the coming weeks, will work hard to ensure that no flowers will emerge for another year. Nobody remembers the exact colour of the flowers. But then it's over ten years now since the first turkeys invaded the garden. Why they should be so keen on clematis is not clear. Nevertheless there is no doubt that it is every turkey's favourite.

The vegetable garden is another area that attracts the attentions of the turkey flock. Although being further from the house, it is generally not until the end of October that the birds will venture that far. They have no preference for any particular vegetable - they like to have a little peck at each one. Obviously they have an innate awareness of the need for a balanced diet.

But by Christmas all these minor inconveniences will have been forgotten. With few crops or animals to sell and all the livestock to feed, the winter months are a bleak time financially for the farmer. So an injection of cash just before Christmas is very welcome. The turkeys will finance the festive season.

The day before Christmas Eve is the time our customers come to collect the

MISTS AND MELLOW FRUITFULNESS . . .

birds. Not before eleven o clock as the local turkey pluckers have to clean out the turkey inners first. The plucking is done five or six days before Christmas but cleaning out their insides livers, giblets and other bits and pieces has to be left till just before they are collected.

Our pluckers are not the tidiest of men. In no time at all the kitchen resembles the site of an illegal cockfight as the corpses are piled high on every available surface. The morality of raising animals for slaughter is not a topic to mention at this sensitive time. Suffice to say that a proselytiser for vegetarianism would be delighted to book the kitchen at this time for a talk. And there would be no need for him to bring his slides.

But as soon as the pluckers have finished walking dirt and feathers into the kitchen floor and are on the way to the pub with their wages, the kitchen is returned to its normal pristine condition. Usually just in time before the first of our well-heeled customers appears. Loyal customers who have come to depend on us to provide the centrepiece of their Christmas table as much as we rely on them to finance ours.

As the day advances, the pile of carcasses becomes smaller and the wad of notes in the kitchen drawer becomes progressively bigger. Various family debts and promises to children are paid off. Christmas Eve may seem a bit late to commence your Christmas shopping but its amazing how you can get it all done if you have prepared your itinerary well in advance and manage to get into town early enough.

It may be psychologically unsound for the farmer to be thinking of December as he gathers in his hay. But without doing so there would be no turkey on the table on Christmas Day. And certainly for the farmer, no bottle of wine to go with it.

20
THE SOUNDS OF SPRING

Doctors tell us that spring is the most stressful time of the year for many people. It's certainly true for farmers. In spring everything needs doing on the farm. It's the time for lambing, calving, hatching, ploughing, sowing and everything else. It's that time of the year when it seems that grass will never grow and the stock will never get out of the shed. A time for worrying that you won't have enough hay to keep your animals alive till the spring brings the fields back to life again. And it's a time to be concerned about money, because for most farmers it's several months since they had anything to sell.

For the sheep farmer with young lambs the big worry is the fox. Spring is a hungry time for foxes and a few new born lambs will quickly fill a hole in a pregnant vixen's stomach. Lights are one way to keep the fox away at night. But you need a lot of them to brighten a big field.

However, in recent years many farmers have discovered that the fox doesn't like the radio. If they leave a radio playing in the field all night then the fox will keep well away. It doesn't seem to matter what station or programmes you leave on. The fox seems to hate 'Book at Bedtime' just as much as 'The World Tonight'. But most farmers tune to music stations for fox control. This is partly because stations such as Radio 1 or Atlantic 252 usually generate a lot more noise than others. But it's also because these stations broadcast all night.

It can be disconcerting for any late night reveller walking home from the local pub to hear the sounds of Oasis or Michael Jackson wafting across the darkness. (For some it is disconcerting to hear these sounds at any time !) At least one local drunk fell to his knees and confessed all, the first time he

We seem to have lost our bus — big yellow thing we left parked by one of these fields of rape...

head singing in the fields. He's now in the front seat for every religious service held within a radius of ten miles. Another individual who passed a field during a talk show was convinced the sheep had been given the gift of speech and saw this as a sign of the impending demise of the entire world. (If sheep did talk would it be with BBC accents?) Anyway, upsetting the local insomniacs is one of the risks the radio-playing sheep farmer has to take.

It has to be a big radio playing in the field. Otherwise, the sound of the wind or heavy rain might drown it out. And it's important to put the radio in a plastic bag. Farmers who use 'audio repellents' have quickly discovered that a wet radio makes no sound. Of course nobody has bothered to find out if the sheep like having the radio on all night. Does it interfere with their sleep? How does a ewe feel about giving birth to the strains of disco music? Do they find the 'News' as frightening as the rest of us? And what about the lambs? What sort of noisy world do they think they are coming into?

At least one local flock didn't like listening to the radio. For when the farmer went out to check the flock in the early morning he discovered the instrument was gone. It was very windy so at first he thought that his small transistor had been blown away. He searched the surrounding hedgerows and ditches without success. For a time he even suspected his neighbours of stealing it. However, later in the day when the wind had died down, he heard the sound of music playing again. But as he searched around the field for the radio, the source of the music seemed to keep moving. As soon as he'd get to the place where he thought the music was coming from, it seemed to come from somewhere else. For a long time he remained perplexed. Eventually he noticed that the sound always seemed loudest when he stood close to a particular black faced old ewe.

What particular song drove the ewe to eat the radio will never be known. I'm sure we all would have our own suggestions. What is certain is that as long as the batteries hold out, one old ewe is literally going to have her bellyful of music. And her lambs will be the most musically educated sheep ever born.

HOW NATURE SIGNALS THE ARRIVAL OF SPRING

21
RABBITTING ON

The popular perception of rabbits is that they are playful furry creatures that come out in numbers at Easter. Farmers have a less benevolent view. To them, these less than loveable creatures are pests that come out in great numbers at all times of the year and are a constant menace to crops.

They do their most obvious damage in the vegetable field. Surprisingly in a field of mixed vegetables the only one that is safe from the rabbit is lettuce. They will nibble your carrot tops, trample down your french beans and dig up your cabbage plants, but contrary to all the exotically illustrated and expensive children's books, they have no interest in lettuce.

They will invade your field early in the morning before you are up or late in the evening when you are safely indoors. They won't just take a few vegetables for themselves and go away. They prefer to take a bite out of as many plants as they can. Farmers could tolerate rabbits if they were at all reasonable in their demands.

If they are a serious problem the only solution is to fence them out of the field. The height of the fence is important to the success of the fence as a deterrent. The farmer who invested in four hundred yards of 3ft high chicken wire quickly discovered that rabbits can jump as high as 5ft. But had the fence been high enough he would have also learned that the rabbit can burrow under the fence as well. At least a foot and a half of the fence needs to be underground.

For many years rabbit farming was the current agricultural fad. But these rabbits were securely housed and fenced. Which of course didn't suit the rabbit. Many of them responded to their unnatural confinement by eating each other. Later the farming flavour of the month was deer farming. That lasted until farmers realised that they would have to borrow fencing from the local prison to keep the animals in.

Another fad was snail farming. With several thousand on a tenth of an acre, trying to count them without stepping on them was a nightmare. They are not very affectionate animals either. But their lack of warmth may be due to the fact that everybody squirms and makes faces when they see them. About the only thing that could be said for them is that they are very

Thirteen thousand five hundred and eighty-three, thirteen thousand five hundred and eighty-four...

quiet animals. They don't moo, baa, or cackle at feeding time. And they are lovely with a light dressing of garlic.

The latest fad is ostrich farming. Not the most attractive of animals, ostriches look a bit like stretched turkeys. Grazing in the field, they look ridiculously out of proportion and give the impression that they would be blown over with the next breath of wind. At a cost of fourteen pounds a pound, few of us will ever know what they taste like. But I'm told the flavour is something like a mixture of turkey and horse. Unfortunately that information only gives most of us half an idea of their taste.

You could become rich if you could predict the next fad. For it is those who get into the new novelty first and sell to other gambling farmers who always seem to make the most money. The later arrivals are usually still busy building up their stock when the public fashion has moved elsewhere.

Elephants seem like unlikely contenders for the next taste sensation. Anyway those beasts would probably knock down your house as well as your fencing. And just by looking at them you can tell that only those with the strongest of teeth could hope to digest them. Something smaller and easier to manage would be preferable. Which is why it's such a pity that everybody is so much against the rat. Every farmer could collect hundreds of them without any effort or alteration to his farm. And the idea of selling something we have plenty of and don't want is very attractive.

For vegetable farmers marketing greenfly would be an attractive proposition. Then we could leave the rest of the vegetables to the rabbits and simply harvest the fly from the lettuce...

'...and verses 2,4,6 and 8 sung by the male voices only.'

22
BORN AGAIN FARMERS

Goats are not so plentiful these days. But if you do see one it is generally a sign that there is a born again farmer in the area.

These new breed of farmers or smallholders are a type of urban refugee. People who are disillusioned with life in the major cities and are prepared to exchange it for a simpler lifestyle on a few acres of land. Their way of life can be described as wholesome or frugal depending on your point of view. They grow their own vegetables and keep a few hens. And of course, milk a few goats.

Some locals wrongly refer to them as New Age hippies. Some even see them as peddlers of drugs and proponents of frightening levels of immorality. Seldom from farming backgrounds, the ideas on agriculture and the environment of these new style 'born again farmers' range from the fanciful to the exotic.

Freed from the routine of city life they embrace all ideas on alternative lifestyles and beliefs with the zeal of the convert. Acupuncture, Herbalism, Home education, Biodynamic agriculture, Permaculture, Tarot cards and Homeopathy are just a few of the systems of belief that they devour with startling ease. Curiously, many of them are against contraception. Which might explain the large clatter of small children that are usually to be found on their holdings.

Some of them see themselves as setting an example for the rest of the world. They view their lives as a blueprint for a faltering humanity to follow. This can be very irritating if they come to visit you. They will shriek with horror when they see your poisonous washing up liquid. They will decline your offer of tea with disdain and wonder aloud why you don't make your tea from various health filled weeds as they do. They will frown at the preposterous notion that you can be a proper father or mother and have a job as well. Although they will never bother to tell you how you can

That ghost train's late again!

finance your children's education without one. If you smoke, they see it as their duty to fan the air energetically even before you light your cigarette. Some of them will even have the arrogance to request that you refrain from smoking in your own living room.

But they are well-meaning souls. Even though having cut themselves off from the mainstream of life they seem further committed to severing their increasingly tenuous links with reality. While they are usually very happy and positive individuals their view of what has become to them, an alien world, is negative and depressing. They see everything such as unusual planetary movements, downturns on the stock exchange or best of all, serious natural disasters, as signs of the impending demise of humanity. It's as if having decided to turn their backs on modern life they would welcome its end to justify their decision.

Their commitment to their chosen brand of sustainable agriculture is generally considerable greater than their knowledge of farming. Hence the goats. Apart from deer, goats are the most difficult animals to keep at home – their milk has a very strong taste and a hairy smell, you can't sell their kids and eating them requires that you have a level of hunger which is thankfully never reached in this fortunate part of the world. But as all the children of these born again farmers are allergic to most foods and all modern processes including pasteurising, the goats have to be kept.

Given the rather gamey taste of goat it's fortunate that most of the born agains are vegetarians. Their staple diet is their own home produced vegetables. The surplus they sell to local shops to provide a supply of what must be badly needed cash. The range of vegetables they grow tends to be as exotic as their philosophies. As a result many local farmer's wives, familiar only with carrots, cabbage and onions are rather suspicious of their Kohl Rabi, Chinese leaves, and Chicory. However it is a tribute to modern marketing methods that one German smallholder managed to sell half an acre of nettles in the health food section of his local supermarket. That he achieved this by giving the nettles a very long fancy foreign name which prompted health conscious customers with high disposable incomes to believe that the oddly familiar plant must be good for them, in no way diminishes his achievement.

On the subject of child rearing, the born agains can be very dogmatic. Modern schools are no place to send your children. Apparently such institutions only develop one side of the brain.

All those years spent by teachers in university renders them totally unfit to educate children, except on one side. Children are better off being educated at home among the plants and the animals. How their alternative children will face the 21st century without the benefit of the increasingly necessary qualifications required by modern society or indeed without any experience of living in it, is never adaquately explained. Once I raised the question in a very mild and roundabout way with one such mother who was cleaning out her henhouse with two trailing goats, several cross-bred dogs and one infant on the breast. Suffice to say I won't ask again.

Modern hospitals are no places to have children either. Children are happier if they are born at home on the kitchen table in front of an invited audience of family and friends. I've never been invited to such occasions but I understand that in some cases the captive audience is required to loudly push and heave in harmony with the mother to assist the child's smooth transition into the world.

But these modern pioneers bring to the countryside a cultural diversity that is frequently lacking in communities exclusively populated with country and western farmers. And they bring to rural conversations, which are generally limited to the weather and the crops, a new topic of interest and endless scope for wild speculation. Especially those who live together in alternative communities. If half the rumours of what goes on in such places are true, and if their social arrangements are as flexible as is widely supposed, then by comparison the love-ins of the sixties were as mild as a Sunday school outing.

Communities should be the ideal way to live. Especially for farmers who only have small children and therefore never have enough help when they need it. It should also be a great place for those who hate housework. For example, in a community of fourteen adults, although washing the dishes would be a gigantic undertaking, it would only be your turn once a fortnight. And provided you didn't stay there forever, you might never have to cook the Christmas dinner.

In theory, on a community farm the responsibility for the house and farm is shared by everybody. In reality human nature being what it is, communities inevitably reach a point where nobody claims responsibility for anything. Then, endless sets of rules have to be made and life in the community becomes even more restrictive than it is in the world the community was intending to replace. Judgements about whose turn it is to empty the compost bucket, lock up the hens, answer the phone, clean the bathroom, keep the children amused and all the other minutiae of daily life have to be discussed at great length and in a rising atmosphere of hostility at endless community meetings. Such meetings tend to distract the community from its original lofty ambition of sharing and togetherness.

Later, as all semblance of togetherness disappears from the community, communication itself breaks down. The communal meal, if cooked, becomes a sparse affair with most residents preferring to eat and sulk in their own rooms. At this point the walls of the house and yard become littered with poignant notes bearing such heart felt pleas as 'would you mind not letting your children walk on my beans' or more dramatic messages such as 'Your cow is sick – I think she's dying'. Notes such as 'Who stole my red biro?' or 'Helmut, I know you are eating white bread – I saw the crumbs on the table' bear witness to the seething anger that is undermining yet another brave experiment in communal living. And of course while all this time consuming and negative activity is going on, the vegetable garden is becoming overgrown with weeds, the crops are not being planted nor the animals cared for. The best hope then is that the impending financial crisis that will be the certain result of this neglect will force the community members to their senses.

Whether you are a born again farmer or a native of muck, life on the farm is far from the romantic ideal that is the view of those who contribute to glossy country magazines. But if you choose to go farming be careful who you choose to bring with you. And unless you are the most biddable and pliable of characters, think long and hard before joining a community farm. After all, one of the reasons for moving to the country is to have your own space, both physically and mentally. An overcrowded community farm can be as stressful as any overcrowded city.

CRICKET ON THE GREEN

23
PASS THE GRAVY
...and Spare a Thought for the Turkey

Turkeys occupy a fairly low place in the order of animals loved by man. Although probably a few places ahead of the rat, the only time of the year that they are viewed with anything close to affection is when they are at rest on our plates on Christmas Day, smothered in gravy. Even then, the number of people who tell you that they really don't like turkey and only get one because of the festive season, continues to be both a testament to the illogicality of the human race and a source of some considerable concern to turkey producers.

Cats and dogs are obviously the animals best loved by humans. Try suggesting serving up a dog or cat for Christmas and confirmation of this fact will be swift and decisive. Horses also receive similar veneration in this country, although gourmets on the continent clearly have a different view. Fish are probably the only animals we seem happy to keep as pets without them becoming any less popular as an adjunct to chips.

Producers of turkeys are asked many times by their customers coming up to Christmas, 'how will the turkey come?' While many are tempted to tell them that their purchase will come 'tied to a piece of string so that they can walk him or her home', the question reflects a fear on the part of the customer that the turkey might actually look like one when they come to collect it. It might have feathers and a head. It might even look at them and make a noise. Worse again, it might attack them and do them an injury – a fairly reasonable response given the circumstances. So to protect the customer from any such fears, most turkeys are sold oven-ready. That is without heads, feet, feathers, movement, or anything else that might suggest that they weren't always meat.

Turkey names

If the farmer is the type that likes to give names to all his animals, then he would be wise not to mention this to his customers.

GOBBLE
GOBBLE
GOB
GOBBLE
GOBBLE
GOBBLE

Sentences such as 'Here's Teresa, she's been looking forward to meeting you – I told her last week you were coming – I really think she understood', are guaranteed to have a more devastating effect on sales than any outbreak of salmonella. And the farmer who advertised in the local paper promising 'a Free colour photo of Your Very Own Turkey as she was on the night before she went to heaven' should not have been surprised at the sudden increase in vegetarianism that ruined his market. Even the local priest, who always bought the biggest one every year, cancelled his order. Although, to be fair, the priest, being of mountain farming stock was not in any way squeamish about the photo. He explained to the unfortunate farmer that he was eating nut roast for Christmas as 'a protest against the theological inaccuracy of his advertisement'.

If his customers are collecting their birds from the farm, then the farmer must be sure to have cleared the yard of feathers, lest the sight of them blowing like snow flakes in the cool December breeze might offend any super-sensitive purchaser. All the heads and twice as many feet should be taken away or if not, securely hidden from view. A bag of heads left casually outside the front door, – their startled eyes staring out at the approaching customers, – would be bound to have a dramatic effect on the more impressionable buyers.

Pets?

Turkeys are not the most affectionate of animals, they don't purr or jump up on your lap. They won't run aimlessly after sticks or nip round to the local shop to collect the newspaper. They certainly won't respond to any ridiculous name you might choose to give them and they are completely impossible to house-train.

On the other hand they won't attack the postman or get the neighbour's dog pregnant. You won't have to take them for a walk as they are intelligent enough to do that all by themselves. And, although they are birds, it is to their eternal credit that they are incapable of constantly repeating any senseless collection of words you might endeavour to teach them. So it's a mystery that nobody considers keeping a turkey as a pet.

One great advantage of a pet turkey is the fact that you will never have to advertise it as an unwanted Christmas present. If he starts to get on your nerves you can simply stick him in the oven. (Although in the interests of fair play it might be better to start by threatening him first.) The other thing to remember is that the turkeys you see at Christmas are only a few months old. So before getting one, be sure to check the capacity of your oven. There's no sense in attempting to discipline him with idle threats. A year old turkey can weigh as much as seventy pounds!

24

TEST YOURSELF
Are you suited to farming and country life?
– the following test will measure your credentials

You hear a cock crow outside your window at 6 am. Do you

(a) pull the blankets over your head and make a mental note to find that recipe for chicken soup?

(b) open the window and throw the bedside locker at him?

(c) immediately jump into your shiny green boots and go to work?

You are sitting down to dinner when a neighbour rings to tell you that your cattle are in his field. Do you

(a) answer in a female voice, say your husband is out and would he mind running them back for you?

(b) advise him to improve his fencing to keep them out in future?

(c) take your napkin off your neck and nip round immediately with half a dozen of your biggest cabbages as a peace offering?

A group of undesirable looking ramblers are picnicking in your field. Do you

(a) warn them to be careful as you've spread poison there last week?

(b) ask them to give you a shout if the bull gets restless?

(c) get the wife to sell them some of her so-called fairy cakes?

You are getting ready to go to a party when you notice that one of your cows is about to give birth. Do you

(a) wish her luck and carry on brushing your mohair jacket?

(b) leave her your phone number?

(c) put the jacket away for another year and get your boots out?

One of your ewes keeps breaking out of the field. Do you

(a) take her aside and gently explain to her that she is being very naughty?

(b) join her front legs to the back with a short rope so she can only travel in circles?

(c) throw her into the boot of your car and drive her to the butcher?

A regular customer complains that your eggs are

That's one more my side - makes it 5-4 to me!

too small. Do you

(a) tell her to boil two at a time?

(b) explain to her that you'll find the particular hen and have her put down?

(c) use a smaller box for her eggs next time she comes?

A neighbour's heifer has been in your field for over a week. Do you

(a) send him a bill for a week's grazing?

(b) check there is nobody looking and run the beast onto the road?

(c) take no action just like your neighbour did last year when your sheep ate his wife's dahlias?

Your Score

Only those with all c's should consider a career in farming or life in the country. Without that unique combination of rural cuteness, gentle tolerance and agricultural arrogance you'd be better off sticking to your window boxes and an occasional visit to the zoo.

If you are really disappointed then treat yourself to a few extra models for your lego farm kit. Or do the quiz again and give the proper answers this time.

25

TEST YOURSELF...AGAIN

How Green is your Lifestyle?

Now that you are all packed and ready for the country you need to check if your way of life is environmentally pure enough for mucking around in the new millenium.

CHECK YOUR GREEN CREDIBILITY RATING

Q1 How often do you eat white bread?

(a) Never
(b) Only when offered some by non-green friends.
(c) I am eating some at the moment with irradiated 'extra sugar' strawberry jam.

Q2 What do you normally eat for breakfast?

(a) Organic muesli with added granola and goats milk.
(b) Barleycup or decaffeinated coffee from a third world co-operative.
(c) Streaky rashers, sausages, fried bread and black pudding.

Q3 You have guests in for dinner who are deeply committed to organic food. Do you . . .

Ah well, Spring is just around the corner.

(a) apologise for running out of organic wine, bread, soup, cheese, etc?
(b) pretend everything is organic and grown by yourself, including the bananas?
(c) serve them several large helpings of organic parsnips and congratulate them on their commitment to saving the planet?

Q4 What is your marital status?

(a) Living with a partner but not sharing his/her name.
(b) Living with a partner but not sharing his/her sleeping bag.
(c) Living in a community and sharing everything.
(d) Can't get on with anybody.

Q5 When washing dishes, do you . . .

(a) use Fairy Liquid?
(b) use one of those environmentally-friendly liquids which only seem to work on dark brown dishes?
(c) give them to the dog to lick clean?

Q6 A local farmer is preparing to cut down a

THE VILLAGE FÊTE

plantation of mature oak trees. Do you . . .

(a) complain bitterly to your friends at work?
(b) lie down in front of his chain saw?
(c) nip round and ask him if he will sell you some cheap firewood?

Q7 Do you smoke?

(a) Of course not, what a ridiculous question. How could anybody in the green movement engage in such a vile and disgusting habit. What about passive smoking etc. etc. etc. Blah Blah Blah. Bladder Bladder Bladder.
(b) Er . . . yes

Q8 Where do you and/or your partner have babies?

(a) At the local hospital with the rest of the unenlightened
(b) At home in my kitchen
(c) Underwater.

Q9 Assuming your baby survived its initial experience as a submarine, what do you use for nappies?

(a) recycled copies of the Green Party's Manifesto
(b) Organic moss and/or dried leaves (in season)
(c) We place him/her directly on our wooden compost bucket
(d) I'd have to ask the wife.

Q10 You are in a pub for a quiet drink. A member of your local green commune recognises you and commences to give you a comprehensive account of his latest compost heap. Do you . . .

(a) smile sweetly and suffer?
(b) burst all the crisp bags you can find?
(c) suggest it's his turn to buy a round?

Your Score

Q1 (a) 5 (b) 2 (c) 0 You can use the jamjar as a night light.

Q2 (a) 5 You must have good teeth (b) 2 Politically sound but little nourishment (c) 0 It smells good sizzling on the pan and tastes even better so it can't be good for you.

Q3 (a) There's no virtue in being mean (b) 4 (c) 3 Is that all you can grow?

Q4 (a) 5 Very typical (b) 0 Highly unusual (c) 0 Have you ever met any of these people? (d) 2

Q5 (a) 0 It's politically incorrect to use the word 'fairy' (b) 5 (c) 1

Q6 (a) 0 (b) 5 Don't forget to wear your green wellies (c) 0

Q7 (a) 5 (b) 25 If you are a smoker and still remain in the green movement with all the self-righteous abuse you regularly receive then your commitment is beyond dispute.

Q8 (a) 0 (b) 3 (c) 0 Well OK, award yourself two marks if it was only a very shallow bath.

Q9 (a) 4 (b) 5 (c) 7 Only if you empty the bucket at least once a week (d) -5

Q10 (a) 0 (b) 3 (c) 5 Cruel, I know, but it's the only sure way to get rid of him.

Your Green Credibility Rating

Over 30 HIGH You probably bore the face off everyone you meet but your credibility is beyond reproach. Check the weather forecast before you sell your suburban semi and move your family into a tree house. Dig out that dirty old green anorak you used to wear on CND marches - you'll need it when you are out of your tree. And lay off the rest of us who can still enjoy our hamburgers.

10 to 30 AVERAGE Thought you would be in the top group? Try practising some of what your preach. Sell the car and get yourself a bicycle, start a vegetable plot and stop drooling over the frozen food counter in supermarkets. Saving the planet requires more of a commitment than declaring your house a nuclear free zone and separating your clear wine bottles from the coloured ones.

0 to 10 LOW The ultimate poseur. You still think that recycling is going home the same way on a bicycle, wheatgerm is a cereal killer and Windscale a large bottle bank? Are you a government minister?

"You and your parsnip wine"

26

A FARMER'S DICTIONARY

Technical terms commonly used in modern agriculture

Cow: Once the most popular of farm animals - now greatly feared in case they get into our hamburgers and drive us crazy. Like milkmen, cows provide milk every day even when it is not required. However, if there were no cows, all coffee would be black, all children would have brittle bones and cornflakes would be too noisy to eat.

Donkey: Smaller than a tractor or a horse, the donkey is considerably less successful as an efficient means of transport. It lacks the natural sense of direction of a tractor and the biddable nature of a horse. The donkey played a significant role in the Christmas story at Bethlehem. However some recently discovered manuscripts suggest that it was in fact Cairo that was the donkey's intended destination. Donkeys make random hiccupping noises called braying which can terrify even the most persistent of ramblers.

Dung: Waste products from farm animals. In cattle it comes in the form of circular pats about the size of a frisbee. Sheep dung is much smaller and resembles a generous portion of black peanuts. By contrast, the waste from hens, ducks and geese is indescribable.

Farming: An occupation similar to zoo-keeping except that on a farm most of the animals are edible and qualify for E.U. grants.

Field: In the academic world, an area of study or research. In farming, a piece of land of variable size similar to a garden but without a house.

Goat: Status symbol for all those who have exchanged well paid graduate employment for a life on the land. Goatkeepers, like their charges, generally sport long beards and are affectionately referred to as hippies.

Like everything with a strong unpleasant taste, goat's milk is very good for you. However, the meat of the goat is considerably less popular on account of its rather high and gamey taste which is said to be similar to that of a horse but with a more persistent odour. Occasionally goats have accidentally mated with sheep. Depending on the locality, the product of this union is known as a geep or a shoat. Being neither one thing nor another, geeps/shoats have no commercial potential.

Hay: Long stems of dried grass. For some unknown reason during the war years, hay fields were considered to be ideal locations for courting and lovemaking. This was before the discovery of 'hay fever'. Nowadays, to discourage promiscuity, the grass is stuffed into large and uncomfortable black plastic bags. These passionless plastic eyesores are called silage.

Horse: A form of transport in some countries – a delicacy in others. Successful race horses are the ones who are frequently

kept aware of the possibility of a less attractive alternative career on the continent.

Old MacDonald: Formerly successful and much loved farmer who kept one of everything on his farm. Forced out of business in the seventies as a result of E.U. policy of specialisation. Now working in the manure management section of London Zoo.

Pig: If you are fond of a hearty fry-up for your breakfast then a pig is a must on your farm. Those greasy goodies that sizzle on the pan and splatter the walls of your kitchen are all parts of the body of a (hopefully) dead pig. From this long naked looking animal come rashers, sausages and black and white pudding. In fact the pig's only failing is that he can't provide the egg as well. However with current rapid advances in biotechnology it will only be a matter of time before pigs can lay eggs and probably even provide a few slices of fried bread to mop up the yolk.

Sheep: Those woolly farm animals constantly being mislaid by Bo. Peep. Believed to be a cure for insomnia if present in sufficient numbers. The size of the flock required to overcome sleeplessness depends on the severity of the problem but can reach astronomical proportions.

The black variety of sheep are used to symbolise those of us who fall out of favour with family, friends or society.

Silage: See under Hay.

Tractor: A mechanical substitute for a horse or several men. Developed since the abolition of slavery. Like the horse, a tractor is sometimes difficult to get started and inevitably breaks down when there is hay to be saved and rain is forecast.

Also bought as status symbols in which case it's important to the status seeker that his new shiny machine is wider than the widest gate on his farm.

Turkey: Popular Christmas dish. Can be very dry if served without generous quantities of gravy. Apart from their annual appearance on a plate once a year, turkeys have no other useful function. They make poor companions, have no discernible intellectual capacity and their feathers will litter the farmyard for months after they've gone. More popular abroad where they've even had an entire country named after them.

Weather: Inexhaustible source of conversation for farmers and country folk. There are really only four main types of weather - wet, dry, sunny and dull. When you have decided which category fits the particular day it is your duty as a country dweller to inform everyone else. It is assumed that nobody else has the same basic powers of observation as yourself and will never notice what sort of a day it is unless they are fortunate enough to meet you and be given the benefit of a full meteorological description.

It's the only cool place for miles!

THE HARVEST FESTIVAL